Bright

A Plante. . . ...

Malaya 1948-56

Campbell Dykes Aitkenhead

Pen Press

First published in Great Britain by Pen Press

All paper used in the printing of this book has been made from wood
grown in managed, sustainable forests.

ISBN 978-1-78003-627-4

Printed and bound in the UK
Pen Press is an imprint of
Indepenpress Publishing Limited
25 Eastern Place
Brighton
BN2 1GJ

A catalogue record of this book is available from
the British Library

Cover design by Karen Aitkenhead

For my daughters

ACKNOWLEDGEMENT

I wish to express my gratitude to Ann and Sandra for all their support and especially Karen for her help in producing this book.

ABOUT THE AUTHOR

Campbell Dykes Aitkenhead was born in Calcutta in 1924, he and his family moving to Australia for a number of years before returning to their original home in Scotland. He attended Websters Seminary in Kirriemuir, Angus, leaving at the age of fourteen to serve as a factory mechanic. His war service began in 1941 when he joined the 2nd Angus Black Watch Home Guard, then the RAFVR, Gordon Highlanders Parachute Regiment until his demob in 1947. Joining Scottish Malayan Estates in Malaya in 1948, he began his career as rubber planter until 1956, when he returned to Scotland to become a fruit farmer and founder of Angus Foods Cannery Ltd. He moved to England with his family in the 1970s and started Biltonglow Ltd, Urethane Foam Systems and retired in 1990 and lives in Sussex.

BACKGROUND

When I set off for Malaya in 1948, as a young man of 23, I had no knowledge of what was to unfold.

Malaya was a British Colony that was invaded by Japanese Forces during WW2. When Japan surrendered, Malaya almost achieved Independence but the British managed to return with the proviso that Independence would eventually be gained. Wanting to secure self-government on their own terms, an independent fight for freedom (Merdeka) by the Malays, and a Communist uprising made up of Chinese *and* Malays brought the country into a complex war against the British. The British Government, having just fought a world war, now played down the significance of further conflict. The Malayan uprising was given the title of 'Malayan Emergency'.

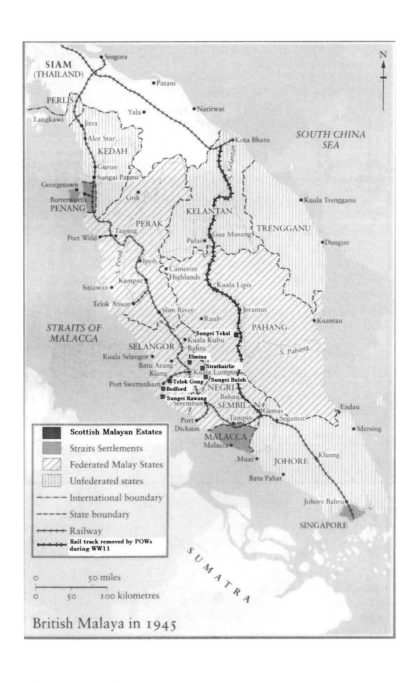

N

SIAM
(THAILAND)

• Singora

• Patani

PERLIS

• Yala

• Naritwat

Langkawi

Jitra

• Alor Star

KEDAH

• Kota Bharu

SOUTH CHINA
SEA

• Gurun

• Sungai Patani

Georgetown

Grik

• Kuala Trengganu

Butterworth

PENANG

KELANTAN

Taiping

PERAK

Pulai

• Gua Musang

TRENGGANU

Port Weld

Ipoh

• Dungun

S. Perak

Kampar

Cameron
Highlands

Kuala Lipis

Sitiawan

Telok Anson

Slim River

• Raub

Jerantut

PAHANG

• Kuantan

STRAITS OF
MALACCA

Sungei Tekal

Kuala Kubu
Bahru

S. Pahang

SELANGOR

Elmina

Kuala Selangor

Strathairlie

Batu Arang

Kuala Lumpur

Klang

Telok Gong

Sungei Buloh

Port Swettenham

Bedford

NEGRI

Sungei Rawang

Bahau

• Endau

Seremban

SEMBILAN

Gemas

Tampin

Segamat

• Mersing

Port
Dickson

MALACCA

Malacca

JOHORE

Kluang

Muar •

Batu Pahat

Johore Bahru

SINGAPORE

	Scottish Malayan Estates
	Straits Settlements
	Federated Malay States
	Unfederated states
--·--·--	International boundary
--- ---	State boundary
+++++	Railway
++++++	**Rail track removed by POWs during WW11**

0 ——— 50 miles

0 —— 50 —— 100 kilometres

S U M A T R A

British Malaya in 1945

INTRODUCTION

Malaya 1948–56

I had told stories about my sojourn in Malaya as a Rubber Planter 1948–56 and listeners often looked at me in disbelief. However some, most of them with similar experiences, suggested that I should record them. In 1958 the late Colonel McKenzie of Almondbank, Perthshire offered to edit and publish the stories, should I put them to paper. Having left school at fourteen with little interest in literary pursuits, I didn't give it another thought. Similarly some years ago, a friend and son of a pre-war Malayan rubber planter, suggested that I record the events for posterity. Although I made a start at that time, it is only now, with ever more revelations coming to light regarding events in Malaya of those years, that I feel the need to complete the task. The following is an account of my life during that time. As I revisit those events I realise now, what a challenging and exciting part of my life it was. So here are my stories.

Campbell Dykes Aitkenhead
(age 20)

CHAPTER 1

Demob

Following my demob from the Parachute Regiment in November 1947, I had two jobs in mind that had been offered to me. One was with the Australian Parachute Fire Fighting Service, paying £20 per week basic salary plus £100 for every parachute jump over a bush fire. The other was with a Company called Zoo Guest set up by an ex Para Major. The company captured animals from all parts of the world, supplying European zoos. The salary here was £15 per week plus all expenses. All very good wages then.

It was during this time and still enjoying my demob leave (122 days) that an old friend of my father's, Wally Annan paid us a visit. In the First World War, Wally had been a Sergeant in the Fife and Forfar Yeomanry, a volunteer Cavalry Regiment, and was badly wounded at Gallipoli. As a young boy I can remember Wally riding through my hometown of Kirriemuir, (known by the locals as 'Kirrie') he went most places on horseback, and was a master horseman. His horse would negotiate, with ease, the low ceilings and narrow passageways that were characteristic of Kirrie. When he came to visit us, he would ride right up to the front of our house and tap on the window before dismounting. I always enjoyed his visits. In his younger days, he was the tenant farmer on 'the Mains of Glamis' near Kirriemuir, best known for being the childhood home of the Queen Mother. Wally had many stories about the place. Wally's sister was the wife of Jock Hunter, the founder of Scottish Malayan Estates and the Strathmore Rubber Company and his nephew was Sir Thomas Weatherspoon, Chairman of the companies. During his visit Wally mentioned that Scottish Malayan were looking for young men to train as Rubber Planters and suggested I go and see Sir Thomas who had a farm, 'The Castleton' at Meigle. This was a good opportunity, being double the pay offered by the other jobs.

Self, front row centre, age 21

Self and 'Ginger' Proctor, Palestine 1945 (self holding cup)

The following afternoon, I borrowed my brother's cycle and set off from Brechin, where our family was staying at the time, for Meigle some 25 miles away. On the way there it was snowing off and on, which made the going slow and by the time I arrived at the Castleton Farm office it was almost five o'clock. Sir Thomas' secretary informed me that Sir Thomas was finished for the day. With that a loud voice shouted, "Who wants to see me?" Sir Thomas appeared from his office. I introduced myself and said, "Wally Annan told me you were looking for young men to train as rubber planters." He led me into his office and asked me a few questions about my army service and told me I would hear from the Directors in Edinburgh in due course.

By the time I left Castleton Farm it was dark and snowing heavily. I thought it best to cycle to my hometown of Kirrie which was only five miles away. In Kirrie I spent the night with the parents of my best friend Angus Herd. Angus and I were both in the RAFVR and volunteered together on the same day in September 1943. He was a Sergeant Air Gunner in the RAF and had been reported missing somewhere over Burma and never returned home. He was nineteen. I think of him often and the remembrance words, 'We will remember them' are especially poignant. I stayed with Angus's parents for a few days, as heavy snowfall continued to keep the roads blocked. During this time I was able to catch up with some old pals.

The following week, back home in Brechin, I received a letter from Scottish Malayan Estates asking me to attend an interview. I went to Edinburgh with my father by train. We called at the George Hotel in George Street for coffee, not far from the Head Office of Scottish Malayan Estates. The head waiter in the George Hotel greeted my father like a long lost brother. He had been the Head Waiter in 1917 when my father stayed at the George for three months as a guest of the Indian Army, whilst receiving treatment for his wounds in an Edinburgh hospital. He had won the MC fighting the Turks in Kut-al-Almara, Mesopotamia, 23rd February 1917, but had been badly wounded. Fortunately he was brought home and it was during his treatment in Edinburgh that he met and was nursed by my mother.

I could see he was enjoying his visit, as the place held many memories for him. Leaving my father at the George, I set off for my interview at 46 Charlotte Square, an imposing Victorian building on one of Edinburgh's main streets.

During the interview, the directors voiced their concerns that I had no agricultural qualifications. I felt it doubtful that they would hire me, but my engineering experience was taken into account and served me well. They also told me that Sir Thomas had mentioned to them about me cycling from Brechin to Meigle and this seemed to impress them, but for a young man in Scotland in those days it wasn't unusual. With the interview over, I was told I would be hearing from them. I went back to the George to join my father and the head waiter for lunch. They were both quite merry by this time and the lunch lasted well into the afternoon.

A week later I received a letter from Edinburgh confirming I had been accepted and a passage to Malaya was being arranged. Part of my contract was that I would spend a few days in the workshops of Jack Oldham, Agricultural Engineers in Coupar Angus. They were agents for the Opperman motor cart of which Scottish Malayan had purchased twelve to replace the old bullock carts on their oil palm estates. I was instructed in how to assemble them. I was to take them with me to Malaya packed in crates and assemble them there.

All the necessary arrangements for the shipment of the motor carts and passage for myself were made with the Glen Line, the ship was the *Glen Ogle* (coincidently, the name of a glen north of Kirriemuir on the Airlie Estate) out of Liverpool. My destination in Malaya was Bukit Cheraka Estate managed by John McGregor.

One of my last duties before leaving home was to pick up a shotgun for John from his wife Ella McGregor of Plovermuir Farm, near Kirriemuir. They had both lived in Malaya during WW2 when Malaya was occupied by the Japanese. I would later learn just what a feisty lass Ella was when I met her again in Malaya some years later.

CHAPTER 2

The Voyage Out

On 20th February 1948 I left Brechin by train for Liverpool to join the *Glen Ogle*, a slow sturdy ship, powered by an experimental diesel engine, the pistons were stationary and the cylinders moved up and down. I arrived too early, some six hours and was not permitted to board ship until it had been cleared by Customs. However, one of the young ship's officers took my baggage, an army kit bag and small grip, saying he would clear them with the Customs Officer and put them in my cabin. I was then free to wander round Liverpool for a few hours. When I arrived back at the ship at 4 p.m. embarkation time, I found my cabin, then went on deck to watch the departure procedure in the floodlit dock. Leaning on the rails, looking over the side, I was tapped on the shoulder – a tall gentleman in a shooting jacket introduced himself as Major General Hunt. He stated, "I believe your name is Aitkenhead and your baggage has been put on my bunk, as we are sharing the same cabin." "Indeed I am," I answered. We walked back to the cabin together, which was directly below the Captain's cabin mid-ship.

Seemingly the young ship's officer had accidentally put my baggage on the top bunk which had been allocated to the General. As I was about to remove my bags the General asked if I preferred the top bunk. "I would," I said. "Good," he replied, "I wet the bed because of a wound I received in 1918 as a young Lieutenant on the Western Front." The General was a straight talker and often very funny. The highest rank I held in the army was acting Lance Corporal unpaid, and this was only for a short period. To share a cabin with a Major General was very odd indeed, however, we did get on well together. He had spent most of his army service in China and was now heading for Formosa (Taiwan). His mission was to secure a contract for the British to install a railway station in and around Formosa and to advise Chiang Kai Shek (the Chinese political and military leader) on the defence of the island against a Chinese Communist attack. In addition to the General and I, there were six other passengers bound for the Far East. The *Glen Ogle* sailed out of Liverpool at 9 p.m. on 21st February 1948.

The first two ports of call were Gibraltar and Port Said. I had hoped we would be stopping at Malta as my uncle Ross was Governor of the Island from 1946–49 and prepared Malta for self-government between 1964–74. For his service he was made Lord Douglas of Barloch. Having been the Labour MP for Battersea 1940–46, he was knighted Sir Frances before becoming Governor of Malta. He was the first civilian Governor of Malta and had control over the military on the Island. The odd thing about this was that during the First World War he was a conscientious objector and served time in prison for his beliefs. He was quite a character and I would have enjoyed meeting him again in Malta.

During the voyage thus far, we had experienced strong winds, driving rain and rough seas so deck games could not take place. Our time was spent playing cards or board games. However, when we reached the Red Sea the Captain had a canvas swimming pool erected on deck, which was a joy to all on board and the usual deck games also commenced. Our teams were the Captain's table versus the Chief Engineer's table. The Captain's table consisted of five ship's officers plus four passengers – Mrs Brown, John Allcock, the General and myself. The Chief Engineer's table had four engineers plus the remaining four passengers. The most popular game was deck golf at which everyone cheated except the General who was my partner. It so happened that he and I were in the finals up against Mrs Brown and the Captain, who were the biggest cheats of all. On this occasion the General noticed me cheating at one hole, he threw in the towel in disgust and made us withdraw from the game, leaving Mrs Brown and the Captain the winners again, as usual. I felt bad about this. We then became spectators, and all was revealed to the General, we never lost a game of deck golf after that. All he said was "two can play at that game" and he became the biggest cheat on board.

The General was an educated man with a keen interest in Egyptology and although he had passed through the Suez Canal on several occasions he had never made a visit to Cairo or the Pyramids. I had spent two years of my army service in the Middle East and had visited many of its great sites. A couple of pals and I had climbed to the top of Giza, the highest of the Pyramids. The General wanted to visit Cairo and as the ship would be in Port Said for at least three days he could make a good tour of it. He asked me to be his guide, all expenses paid, subject of course to the Captain's approval, which was duly given. We caught a taxi at Port Said and made our way down to Cairo where we had arranged to stay at the Sheppard Hotel. It was a trip I had made several times before, the last being only three months prior to me leaving for Malaya. We spent the next two days visiting the Pyramids, Sphinx and museums. The following morning we proceeded to Port Suez, where we spent the night. The *Glen Ogle* docked at Port Tewfik during the night and we rejoined the ship the next day.

Our next stop was Aden, a three-day stay. Quite some time here was spent touring the old city in the crater. The most interesting feature was the nine wells of Aden. A sequence of nine wells built into the crater wall, each one larger in size as they descend. The wells were designed to catch rain – very odd as it never rains in Aden! We then sailed across the Indian Ocean to Colombo, Sri Lanka and berthed for two days. Here I had an old friend of the family to visit, a Tea Planter, Alf Lesley, from Arbroath, who owned a tea plantation up in Mount Kanda. Unfortunately when I arrived at his estate he was away for a few days. From there we sailed on to George Town, Penang, a three-day stay. On the second day I went ashore with the General and the Chief Engineer. Our first call was the European & Orient Hotel for a cool beer. I left them there while myself and one of the ship's officers went sightseeing around George Town. We spent that evening at the 'City Lights' a cabaret situated close to the E & O Hotel.

Back on board ship there was no sign of the General or Chief Engineer and as the saloon was closed I went to bed. Around 2 a.m. the General and the Chief Engineer came into our cabin, they wanted me to join them in a drink. They were both very merry so I pretended to be asleep. I heard the Chief say "come and see the engines," with that the General picked up my dressing gown and they both left the cabin. As usual, the next morning the General was up first, we exchanged greetings and with that he looked at my dressing gown which was covered in oil and asked, "Where were you last night?" I answered, "I know where I was," and left it at that. However that evening I found a new Chinese dressing gown lying on my bunk, the old one having gone.

The seating arrangement at the Captain's table was done alphabetically – the Captain at the head of the table with me on his right, Mrs Brown on his left and the General sat next to me. The Captain was a very quietly spoken man and the General, being slightly deaf, could not hear all that was being said. I offered to exchange seats, but he declined. His plan to overcome the situation was as follows – if the Captain was on a serious subject, I would give him one kick on the leg and he would nod approvingly, if the Captain was joking I would give him two kicks and he would laugh. All very simple and it seemed to work. On one occasion when the Captain was telling a story of the time he was torpedoed during mid-winter and almost perished in an open lifeboat, not paying attention I misjudged for a moment and gave the General two kicks instead of one, he burst out laughing to the horror of the Captain. I immediately explained the situation, and with the Captain's approval the General and I exchanged seats, to the amusement of the other passengers.

The voyage was almost over. When I awoke the ship was lying at anchor in Telok Kelang (Bay of Kelang) awaiting a berth at Port Swettenham. After breakfast a sampan came alongside with two Europeans on board, a voice shouted, "Is Aitkenhead on board this ship?" It was John McGregor, the Senior Planter in the Scottish Malayan Group, he managed the largest rubber estate, some 4000 acres and was to be my boss. His staff consisted of two assistants, Arthur Grant, and Dickie Dickson, one Tamil Conductor (foreman) and two office clerks from Madras. The other European was Jock Elgar, agent for the Glen Line. A gangway was lowered, McGregor and Elgar came on board followed by two Tamil labourers from Bukit Cheraka Estate who were to help me unload my baggage. The two Tamil workers followed me down to the cabin. Arriving back on deck with only a kit bag and a small grip, McGregor shook his head in amazement. Seemingly he had expected me to bring all my necessary household utensils and linen with me. But, there was one more item I had almost forgotten – McGregor's shotgun! It had been held in bond by the Captain. Before leaving Scotland I had packed the gun in my kitbag; how it got through Customs in Liverpool I will never know. When the General had seen it, he had thought it best that the Captain place it in custody during the voyage.

CHAPTER 3
Malaya

I said my farewells to all on board and left with John McGregor. He was a well-dressed man with a stocky build and struck me as being a cross between a ploughman and a banker. We boarded the sampan and entered the Sungai Sangat. I could see, on both sides of the estuary, a vast area of deep green mangrove swamps which came right down to the water's edge; the tide was ebbing and revealed 'Mud-Skippers' – ugly looking fish-like creatures, with large heads and bulging eyes slithering on the oozing mire in and around the exposed roots of the mangrove bushes. Although this dense entanglement of branches and naked roots was an eerie and foreboding sight and one of my first impressions of Malaya, it's one I've never forgotten. Malaya has no clear-cut seasons, the entire landscape is a perpetual green; although beautiful, it was hard to get used to and in the early days I often found myself thinking of my Highland hills of home and the cool vibrant autumn colours of Scotland.

On arrival at the dockside McGregor suggested that I meet up with him later in the station bar as I had to go through Customs first. After the Custom inspection, my baggage was put on the 5-ton waiting estate truck and taken to McGregor's bungalow on Bukit Cheraka Estate and, as arranged, I joined McGregor in the bar. Little did I know then that this was to end up in a long drinking session.

After many beers we left the bar and made our way to the car. At the entrance to the car park there was a satay kedai (shop) and McGregor suggested that I should have my first Malayan meal. He ordered us some satay – the peanut sauce was so hot and spicy that even, starving as I was, I could not eat it. Back in the car, an impressive large American Buick, only Malay was spoken (at this stage I could understand no Malay at all) and the Malay Sais (chauffeur) drove to the Klang Club. Here I met some of McGregor's planter friends.

A Tennis Club Ball was to be held in the club that night, they were making the final arrangements and, of course, more drink to help things along. A planter friend of McGregor's who seemed to be in charge of the festivities was Ted Clyne, a tall overly smart man. Whenever I saw him his tunic and shorts were pressed to a knife-edge, his knee-high socks were snowy white and his shoes were polished to perfection. Even his drinking habits were characteristic of the man. In a ritualised manner he would pour his gin, adding angostura bitters, and after slowly rolling the glass he would produce his personal silver swizzle stick from his shirt pocket and with great deliberation mix his drink. He was renowned throughout the district for his lavish curry tiffins, and an invitation was always gratefully received as an entertaining evening was bound to ensue. He was indeed a Colonel Blimp of the old Raj age. It was said that he had been very badly treated by the Japanese as a POW. No doubt they had not appreciated his arrogant but entertaining manner.

Arriving late in the afternoon at the estate bungalow, more drinks were served! By this time I was feeling very hungry indeed, having had nothing to eat all day. Asking about food I was told, "later, later." Around 7 p.m. McGregor's two assistants – Arthur Grant, a farmer's son from Monifieth and Dickie Dickson an ex-major from Edinburgh – arrived in evening dress. After a wash and change I was more than ready for dinner. We all got into the Buick and were driven back to the Klang Club, arriving too late for dinner as the last course was being served, much to my disappointment! As happened that morning, McGregor insisted on paying for everything – all was to be charged to him. Seemingly, if an assistant was in the company of a manager it was not done for him to offer to buy a drink. This went back to WW1 days when assistants on plantations were nicknamed 'Creepers'. With Scottish Malayan Estates, during their first five-year contract, no salary was paid, hence the assistant had to rely on his manager for food, drink and his upkeep in general. Arthur Grant was the senior assistant and I had to speak to him even regarding food. He in turn would have to obtain McGregor's permission, without which, going out for a meal was not even an option. This was the customary way to go about things. So it was arranged that McGregor would take us out for a Chinese meal "later!"

After several dances we at last went out for the meal, by this time it was around midnight. The only meals available were of course Chinese. In those days there were very few Chinese restaurants in the UK, at least I had never been in one. I had to rely on McGregor to order for me. The meal he ordered was the famous Malay/Chinese 'Mamee' a dish of noodles, prawn, crab, chicken, pork and Chinese greens, the fried egg on top was a British addition. That evening it looked like a dog's dinner to me but I ate every last bit of it! Afterwards we went back to the ball and stayed there until 3 a.m. On the way home we stopped at a Chinese bakery for some fruit balls – a mixture of sticky dough, spice, fruit and mincemeat – this also was not to my liking. I would later come to relish and appreciate Chinese/Malay food, indeed they are my favourites, even to this day. Finally arriving back at the bungalow I went straight to bed tired and hungry. The next morning I was wakened by the 'houseboy' (a term I never liked, especially as most were not young boys at all, but men older than myself) who gave me a tankard of ale and told me that McGregor wanted to see me.

In the lounge I was surprised to see Grant and Dickson still in their dress suits. At that time I did not have a dress suit, and had gone to the ball in my demob suit. They were sitting drinking with McGregor who was wearing a sarong. When I asked about breakfast, I was again told "later – it's a holiday today, the day after pay day."

During my interview in Edinburgh I had asked about the daily working hours. The answer from the Company Secretary was swift and to the point. "If required you will work 24 hours a day, 365 days a year." This was true, up to a point. The estate labour force had one official day off a month, the day after pay day. It just so happened that I had arrived on a pay day, a Saturday, the first Saturday in the month of April 1948, a day I will always remember!

Around midday the Buick pulled up and a Siamese woman with two young girls aged between 14–16 got out and came into the bungalow. McGregor introduced me saying, "This is Jade and these are my two daughters." Having had tea with his wife Ella McGregor, in Kirriemuir a few weeks' back, I took this to be a joke. How wrong I was. Breakfast was cancelled as Jade was to make a Siamese curry which would take about four hours – after all there was no hurry, this was a holiday! At last we sat down to eat, it was 5 pm! Alas again, the curry was not for me, it was far too hot! Jade and her daughters left about 9 p.m. and when the Buick came back, we all went into Klang to visit some of the infamous hotels. I have no idea when we got back to the bungalow.

Waking the next morning, the air was humid and heavy; I

opened the shutters and could see Tamil women tapping rubber trees – an extraordinary sight and my first view of what would eventually become commonplace. I collected my thoughts and was eager to start my first day and joined McGregor who was having brunch in the dining room with the two women we had met in Klang. This was my first decent meal in two and a half days!

During brunch it was decided that the women be dropped off in Klang on our way to Port Swettenham where we would arrange for the collection of the Opperman Motor Carts. On the way back we stopped at the Klang Club for a quick one – however, McGregor got involved with two other planters and I could see the beginnings of another drinking session. One way or the other I had had enough and told McGregor I was packing the job in and making for Australia to take up the Parachute Fire Fighting work. With that McGregor stood up and said, "Well if you want work you'll get work." We left the Klang Club, leaving our drinks on the table.

I was taken to Arthur Grant's where I was to stay for the next ten days. In those days there were no electric lights in any of the bungalows, they were lit by tilly lamps which drew a multitude of insects of every kind. The bungalow water was drawn from a well, drinking water was filtered and boiled, all cooking was done on a wood burning stove. The fridges were of the paraffin type. With high humidity conditions in general and the heat from the lamps and fridge, you were in a constant sweat; mosquitoes didn't help the conditions either and I found it difficult to sleep. Every morning I could see my footprints in the dew on the bedroom floor.

Malaya was very different from anywhere I had travelled. From the moment I arrived, this land and its people captivated me. It is a haven full of exotic plants and succulent fruits. One plant in particular is mimosa which grows to a height of approximately 9 inches and its dense matt foliage can cover a fairly large area. The leaves are delicate, small and fern-like. Should you put your foot two inches above the plant, the small leaves would close up and almost disappear, leaving a stem bristling with sharp thorns. As soon as your foot was removed the leaves would immediately open up.

There is one unusual seasonal variety of bean called Kachang Kuning (yellow bean). This is a long bean which grows on a small tree. When eaten it will stain clothing yellow, especially when perspiring. According to some Pahang Malays, Kachang Kuning is health-giving and helps fight off Malaria.

Another interesting plant is the Durian, a large oblong-shaped fruit about 7–9 inches long with a thorny, thick skin. It grows on a fairly high tree. The flesh of the fruit is indeed very sweet and gives off a strong sickly sweet odour. The Malays believed that the flesh of the Durian was an aphrodisiac and one of their sayings was, 'Durian jatuh sarong naik.' The Durian falls and the sarongs come up!

In conversation Malays would often refer to a proverb or saying. For example to describe someone as 'dua muka' (two-faced) they would say 'ada gula ada semut' – where there is sugar there are ants. For anyone going on holiday their favourite saying was, 'pergi dengan muka gajak mari dengan muka tikus' – go away with face of an elephant, come back with the face of a mouse. This was typical of the enriched language that was used in everyday conversation and served to lighten the hard-working day for all of us.

The normal hours for Arthur were up at 5 a.m. and at 5.30 muster the labour force. The muster roll-call check had to be with McGregor by 6.30 a.m., giving a distribution of the number of workers on each job i.e. tapping rubber, factory work, smokehouse work, packing rubber, weeding, nursery work, cutting out old trees, drainage repair, cleaning lines and the sick list. All this had to be correct as two ledgers were kept, one by Arthur and the other by the office, both had to balance for the accounts and payroll. As soon as it was daylight the daily inspection of work commenced. First, the tapping: this was a delicate procedure which had to be strictly adhered to, for the vigour and prosperity of the rubber tree, come to that, for the estate itself. After this inspection, brunch was between 11 and 12 noon, followed by the weighing in of each tapper's collection of latex and the total weight for the day sent to the office. In the afternoon book keeping was done, followed by the issue of rice and canned milk. All these tasks and many more took place every day, seven days a week.

Bukit Cheraka Estate was split into three divisions. McGregor with a Tamil Assistant on the Home Division, Grant and Dickson on the other outlying divisions, each division having an area of approximately 1300 acres. Unlike most rubber companies, it was company policy for Scottish Malayan not to employ Asian Conductors. (A Conductor was an Asian interpreter with a knowledge of planting.) Scottish Malayan wanted their Assistant Managers to learn Tamil Indian and to gain front line working experience. Their Assistant Managers were thrown in at the deep end and allowed to get on with it. So the quicker you spoke the language the easier the work became.

A workshop was provided at the rubber factory where, with help, we assembled the Opperman Motor Carts, which were sent to the oil palm estates Elmina, Sungai Rawang, Riverside. I took three with me to Sungai Tekal Estate where I was to take up the position of Assistant Manager.

Driver working with Opperman motor cart

On 12th April the three carts were loaded onto flat-top rail wagons at Klang railway station. Goods wagons and passenger carriages were all part of the same train. On the journey up to Sungai Tekal there was one change at a place called Gemas. From Klang to Gemas it was first class and very comfortable; from Gemas north to Sungai Tekal it was third class with open windows and wooden forms, very hard going. The following day, on reaching Sungai Tekal, the flat-top wagons were disconnected from the train and manhandled into the Tekal siding. I was met at the halt by Hamish Middleton, the manager of Sungai Tekal Estate. Middleton had studied at Aberdeen University obtaining a PHD in agriculture. He

24

was quiet and soft spoken and lived with his Chinese girlfriend Betty Lou, whom he adored. His assistant Jimmy Baxter (ex-para Captain 5th Scottish Battalion) from Dundee was in charge of the oil palm division. That evening Middleton and Betty Lou gave Baxter a farewell dinner, they were good company and it was an evening I thoroughly enjoyed. The following morning Baxter handed over the oil palm division to me and was delighted to do so, as this was in a remote outpost of Sungai Tekal, a very isolated and lonely place. He left the estate looking happy and relieved.

Hamish Middleton

During the day I seldom saw Middleton as he managed the rubber division. Occasionally I would see him when I took the rainfall measurements to the main office. Our bungalows were some two miles apart. In those days there were no roads to Sungai Tekal and very few links to the outside world. The estate was isolated and surrounded by dense jungle. Like Baxter before me, I was invited to dinner by Middleton and Betty Lou every Saturday night and that was the only socialising available.

CHAPTER 4
The Emergency Begins

In June 1948 the Malayan Communist Party, having not been given a say in Malayan Government matters, took up arms against British rule. Several planters had already been killed by communist bandits and in view of this planters were commissioned by their District Officers as Auxiliary Police Inspectors. Our mission was to recruit and train a Special Police Force to guard the factories and bungalows on the estate. The only weapons available at the time were single barrel shotguns which the estate purchased and issued to the police recruits. The recruits were all Malays enlisted from local kampongs (villages). Some had experience in the use of the shotgun. Middleton and I had gathered together a private army of some 30 men paid by the estate. Most of the recruits came from the kampongs in and around the Kuala Krau area.

Self and recruits, early in 1949

The manager's bungalow at Sungai Tekal was situated on a bukit (hill) from which one could see the whole estate. It was set in a beautiful garden full of plants shrubs and trees. It had three large bedrooms all en suite with dressing rooms, a large lounge with magnificent views, a large dining room and mosquito-proof reading room. A veranda ran all around the bungalow and all rooms opened on to it. The kitchen and servants' quarters were on the lower level. When the Emergency broke out the bungalow was fortified. All plants, shrubs and trees were removed to give a clear sight for gunfire.

Sungai Tekal was in the state of Pahang which was essentially a 'Malay State' unlike other states whose communist armies were predominantly Chinese. In the early stages of the Emergency over 500 radical Malays, who were demanding freedom from British rule, took to the jungle, forming the new all Malay Regiment of the MNLA (Malayan National Liberation Army) named the 10th Malay Regiment, under the command of Abdullah CD as he liked to be known, CD being the initials of his first name 'Che Dat bin', bin meaning 'son of' – son of Abdullah. He was a very important leader and seemingly wanted his name to portray this. He was a well-educated Malay and during the Japanese occupation had fought with the British 136 Force, like many in the MPAJA (Malayan Peoples Anti-Japanese Army). The reign of terror established in and around the towns of Temerloh and Mentakab by communist terrorists (CTs) ('bandits' as we knew them), was of great concern. The 10th Malay Regiment remained a menace to the British throughout the Emergency.

The Malays we recruited were now on a regular monthly wage and many of them wanted the estate to hold back part of their earnings, as a method of saving. When it was suggested to them that they should open a Post Office savings account and gain interest, they explained that the interest was 'Haram' (forbidden by religious law). They called interest 'bunga wang' (flower money or first fruit money). In those days very little money changed hands in the kampongs.

There were no banks in this area of Pahang and the pay-roll had to be collected from the District Office in Temerloh. However, due to the Emergency this method was too dangerous, so The Chartered Bank of India Australia and China made arrangements with the Selangor Flying Club to have the payroll dropped by air. Having been a pathfinder in the Parachute Regiment, the drop zone was very easy to mark out. On the first drop the money bag burst and the $12,000 monthly payroll was scattered over a large area. When we eventually gathered it together again there were only a few dollars missing. I never knew dishonesty to be a problem amongst the workforce.

Guards with payroll drop

Payroll drop

Payroll plane

After two months the government issued 303 rifles to our force. Britain had just fought WW2, yet the only ammunition available at the time was dated 1923, this was unbelievable. When I got the 303 rifles, I took the Malay recruits down to a home-made rifle range for target practice. While in the progress of explaining the working of the rifle, I lay down to demonstrate the actual shooting at the target. On taking aim, I squeezed the trigger but nothing happened. I re-cocked the rifle and tried again, nothing. On the third attempt there was a puff of smoke and the bullet fell to the ground some three feet from the rifle. So much for the 1923 ammo! We had a bit of fun with this ammo, the drill being: 1) squeeze the trigger, 2) take aim, 3) count to three – and hope for the best. The force went back to shotguns for the time being. It was another two months before new ammunition was issued.

Up to this point there had been several minor incidents with the communist attacks. However, on the night 8th November 1948 a full company of bandits (CTs) attacked the estate, wrecking the rubber factory, burning down two smoke houses, the packing shed and the rubber store. The Malay Special Police guarding the factory compound joined ranks with the communists who then attacked the oil palm factory. Here also, the Malay Special Police joined ranks with the communists and proceeded to wreck the factory, burning down the main office, store and petrol station. They set fire to the new seven-ton Bedford truck and all other motor transport within the factory compound. The truly alarming fact was that the Malay Special Police had joined the communist ranks! This was a devastating blow to the authorities and was immediately hushed up.

In September 1948 two police sergeants (ex Palestine Police, the British mandate in Palestine ended in May 1948) Bob Brown and Jock Finnie were posted to the estate and took command of the Special Force that Middleton and I had recruited. Incidentally, I had met Bob Brown previously in 1947 during my army service in Palestine. On the night of the bandit attack we were all staying at Middleton's bungalow, half a mile away from the factories. When the attack started and we saw both factories on fire, Middleton and Sergeant Brown decided to investigate. It was about 10 p.m. and up to this point no shots had been fired and they felt it was safe to leave by car. At the foot of the bukit leading from the bungalow they ran into a communist ambush. Middleton was shot dead and Sergeant Brown badly wounded in both legs.

When I heard the automatic fire, I decided to investigate and a young Malay, Tan bin Youseff volunteered to come with me. Tan was an enthusiastic volunteer, a little younger than myself, around 18. This left Sergeant Finnie and nine Malay Special Police force to defend the bungalow. Near the bottom of the bukit, Sergeant Brown called out for help from the roadside ditch as we passed by. We carried him back to the bungalow where Sergeant Finnie attended to his wounds. Tan and I went back down to see if we could help Middleton.

When I got near the car, I called out to Middleton several times – there was no answer. One of the red reflectors on the back of the car had broken and was showing a bright light. So before getting closer, I put the light out by firing one barrel from the shotgun I was carrying. At that moment the terrorists opened up with automatic fire. I threw two hand grenades in that direction and the firing stopped. Tan engaged the terrorists to his right which allowed me to approach the car. Middleton was hanging out of the car and I could see he was already dead.

There was nothing we could do, so we made a quick retreat back to the bungalow.

Car shortly after Middleton and Sergeant Brown were ambushed

During the night the bungalow was attacked several times. Each attack was driven off and in the end the terrorists gave up and withdrew. The recently installed old-fashioned telephone system was out of order, the wires having been cut, and the new radio link with Mentakab Police was also out of order. This was a mysterious failure, as all police stations were on full alert and I suspect it had something to do with one or two Malay police stationed at Mentakab. At dawn Tan and I went out and found the spot where the telephone wires had been cut and repaired them with some electrical flex. Contact was then made with Mentakab Police calling for reinforcements. Taking the estate pick-up truck, we drove down and retrieved Middleton's body which had been robbed of his boots and watch. Betty Lou, Middleton's Chinese girlfriend was in a state of shock on seeing his body and we could do very little to comfort her.

I don't know if Middleton made any provision in his will for Betty. I know that, on hearing the dreadful news, Mac Hunter arrived at Sungai Tekal and reassured her that Scottish Malayan would grant her a gratuity. She went with him when he left the estate. Hunter was a firm taskmaster but nonetheless a compassionate man.

Self in the radio room Sungai Tekal

Up to now we had been cut off from the rest of the estate. With Tan and another Malay escort I set off to check on the labour force. When we got to the oil palm compound we witnessed a scene of complete devastation. Most of the labour force had gathered, looking desolate and deeply upset, especially the office staff. I tried hard to console them by saying we would rebuild immediately and for them to make a start now by cleaning up.

Some of the devastation after the bandits' raid

The petrol station was also on fire, this was an unbelievable sight. It consisted of a timber building with a corrugated iron roof, containing 20 x 44 gallon drums of petrol, 10 x 44 gallons of diesel and 2 x 44 gallons of engine oil. The bandits had removed all the bungs from the drums, soaked several gunny (hessian) sacks in petrol, placed them inside and around the station and set them alight. The twin doors and most parts of the wall were burnt out, but the corrugated iron roof was still standing. The petrol drums were burning or flaming in a way that is very difficult to explain, as the drums were on fire but at different intervals. It was like a very large slow-running petrol engine firing on all cylinders, that is the only way I can describe it. What may have happened was that the heated-up petrol in the drums with their bungs removed were giving off a gas, the flame from one drum was igniting another drum before dying down and recharging with gas, these in turn would ignite again at different intervals and so the cycle continued. This had been going on all night long. It was an incredible sight to watch. We soaked the gunny sacks in water and as the flame from each drum died down we covered the bung-hole with a wet gunny sack, thus extinguishing the fire in each drum. When I think back this was foolhardy, as the drum could have exploded at anytime, but in those days one did not think twice. In addition to the devastation, the bandits had also opened the drain valves on the palm oil storage tanks releasing hundreds of gallons of oil.

Sergeant Brown was still in great pain, although he had been seen by the estate dresser (male nurse). He needed hospital treatment in Mentakab and Middleton's body had to go to the morgue. There were no roads to Sungai Tekal. The only way in and out was by rail; two trains a day ran, one to Mentakab at 9 a.m. and another from Mentakab at 3 p.m. On checking with the Station Master at Kuala Krau, we were told that the down train to Mentakab would be one and a half hours late due to terrorist activity on the line. We made our way to Sungai Tekal Halt, taking great care not to be ambushed, to await the down train from Kuala Krau. However, much to our astonishment the train did not stop and flashed past at top speed. Later we discovered that the engine driver was being held at gunpoint under terrorist threat and told not to stop at Sungai Tekal Halt. It was late afternoon before reinforcements consisting of a platoon of Gurkhas, under the command of Lieutenant Mike Day; two European police sergeants, Bill Lawless and Dave Griffith; together with twelve Malay police and the OCPD (officer in charge of police district) in charge of the Mentakab district arrived, and still later before Brown was taken to Mentakab hospital and Middleton to the morgue.

The next morning Mac Hunter, our Managing Director, arrived having travelled from Mentakab by rail with his full police escort. Surveying the destruction he made his report to the Directors in Edinburgh and advised on restorations to the estate and any work that should take place immediately, giving me a free hand to carry it out. While remedial work was taking place, outside arrangements were made with other estates to have our crops processed. Rubber tapping and oil palm harvesting started within three days of the attack. Repairs to the rubber and oil palm factories were given priority and we were back in full production again within six weeks.

For my services to the company I received a cash reward of $1,000 plus 14 days' local leave with first class travel and accommodation, all expenses paid. Leave respite had to wait until the new manager was appointed. Both Tan and I were recommended for a police medal. However, owing to the political sensitivity and embarrassment regarding the desertion of the Malay Police, the total lack of communication and the late arrival of reinforcements, this disaster was quickly hushed up and the facts kept from the public for obvious security reasons – the recommendation for award of medals were delayed and then forgotten. Also the fact that I had been fined £5 at Forfar Sheriff Court in 1942 for missing Home Guard (Dad's Army) parades, may not have helped matters! The police report on this £5, fine which I did not know about, came to light in later years when I was Manager at Sungai Tekal Estate. At least Tan bin Youseff should have received some form of recognition for his loyalty and the heroic part he played. The communist terrorist attack at Sungai Tekal was the subject of a debate in the House of Commons. I must find out the date on which it took place.

Following the bandits' raid, the special police force on the estate was more than doubled and I was given a personal bodyguard of four Malayan Special Police. There was also a platoon of British troops stationed on the estate most of the time, or within easy striking distance should the estate be attacked again. Because of this new approach by the government, the bandits changed their tactics, which comprised slashing rubber trees, harvesting oil palms, acts of sabotage, especially on the railway line, intimidation of the labour force and of course the deadly ambush. Another favourite pastime was cutting telephone wires, in fact the telephone was out of order most of the time. In view of this, a reliable radio link was established.

In late January 1949 James Robertson was appointed manager of Sungai Tekal with myself as his assistant. It was only then in February of that year I was able to take the 14 days' local leave with all expenses paid as part of my gratuity following the bandits' attack on the estate in November 1948.

CHAPTER 5

Bandits

Myadin

Among those who had joined the communists was an Indonesian man called Myadin, who had served with the Japanese Indonesian Army to rid Indonesia of the Dutch. He was one of the first volunteers we recruited. He was a very intelligent person and likeable with it and we got on well together. With his military knowledge he was quickly promoted to Sergeant. He told me that after the Japanese surrender he had rebelled against the incoming Dutch rule in 1945–46. Coincidently, a dear friend, the late Jim Stalker who served in the navy during WW2, was sent to Indonesia in 1945 to rescue the Dutch from Indonesian Freedom Fighters. Although it was common knowledge that pre-war Dutch rule in Indonesia was severe, Myadin's reasons for rebelling and his account of Dutch planters' treatment of their labour force was shocking. For example, he explained that a planter's bungalow was completely out of bounds to the entire labour force. Should it be absolutely necessary for a labourer to see his manager out of office hours, it was the rule for him or her to crawl on all fours up to the bungalow and wait there in a crouching position till asked to stand. Whipping for bad workmanship was routine. If this were all true, no wonder the Indonesians rebelled against the return of Dutch rule after the war.

On a lighter note, one of the good things the Dutch did was to train the Indonesian engineers in the art of drainage. They became experts and carried out most of the plantation drainage work throughout Malaya. Good drainage was an essential part in the cultivation of rubber and palm oil.

I always had the feeling Myadin knew more than he let on, he was a naturally intelligent person. Perhaps he was an agent for the Communist Party! Sorry to say Sergeant Myadin became one of Pahang's most wanted terrorists.

Wan Ali

November 1948

That night's desertion by the Malays may have been, in part, due to the fact that one of the bandits was the notorious Wan Ali who believed he could only be killed by a silver bullet. It was true that so far he had escaped all efforts to capture him and had been shot at several times. Superstition and folklore were commonplace in those days and many bandits made themselves cult figures famed for their 'invulnerability'.

However in August 1949 the following appeared in *The Straits Times*. 'In a Kampong near Kuala Krau on the Sungai Pahang the notorious bandit Wan Ali who took part in the attack on Sungai Tekal was shot and killed.' There was a price of $10,000 on his head and he was shot dead by Kampong guards. The news flashed all over Malaya. He was killed with buckshot and not the silver bullet he forecast. *The Straits Times* said Wan Ali had boasted of his invulnerability to bullets. It was big news and $10,000 was a lot of money, but in the kampongs all along the Sungai Pahang it was a fortune.

cult" and could only be killed by a silver bullet.

Militant Youth

He started that legend after Japanese guards had shot at him without result when he tried to loot a place during the occupation.

He left a Japanese-sponsored Malay organisation, which had acted as a fifth column during the Japanese invasion and joined the M.P.A.J.A.

After the war, he was an active member of the A.P.I. the militant youth organisation attached to the Malay Nationalist Party. When A.P.I. was banned in 1947, he became a member of the Central Committee of the Communist-sponsored Malay organisation, P.E.T.A. When the emergency started, he escaped into the jungle.

Last November, he took part in the attack on Sungei Tekal Estate, at Mentakab, when the manager was murdered. His latest murder was on June 26 when he shot dead Ahmad Kamaruddin bin Hail Akir, the Penghulu of Pulau Tawar.

Whenever his gang committed a murder or a robbery, he used to shout: "This is Wan Ali."

WAN ALI, the Malay bandit leader who claimed that only a silver bullet could kill him, after being shot dead by Pahang kampong guards near Jerantut on Sunday.—P.R. picture.

ROYAL WEDDING

LONDON, Mon.—The King and Queen are expected to attend the marriage of their nephew, the Earl of Harewood, to Austrian-born Miss Marion Stein on Sept. 29 at the Chapel Royal, Saint James's Palace, London.—Reuter.

Wan Ali, front page, *The Straits Times* 9th August 1949

In pre-war days (1939–45) Sungai Tekal Estate was known to planters and staff of Scottish Malayan as the 'Penal Plantation' as it was situated so deep in the Pahang jungle. It was so isolated that assistants and managers were contracted to serve only twelve months on Sungai Tekal as part of their first five-year agreement. Due to the Emergency I served a long eighteen months. When my first transfer to Elmina Estate in Selangor came through, I was extremely relieved to get back to a more civilised way of life or so I thought, until I was transferred to the back division…

CHAPTER 6
Loneliness and Che Puteh

The takeover in April 1948 from Jimmy Baxter as assistant manager of the oil palm division was a fairly straightforward procedure. It was during this time, when I had finally settled and found my feet on Sungai Tekal, that the problem of loneliness began to torment me, day and especially night as darkness set in. The bungalow was remote and situated on the side of an anak bukit (hillock), between the oil palm factory and the workers' quarters. There was no electric light, telephone or radio. The only other resident was the Chinese cook who could speak no English. The light was from two tilly lamps – one in the kitchen, one in the lounge. They gave off a disagreeable heat, increasing the humidity. The bright light also attracted a multitude of insects and the ceilings of the rooms were overrun with chichaks (geckos – as with many of the Malay words I know, the spellings may have changed, but I am using my original English-Malay dictionary, the pages of which are well-worn!), a small house lizard which fed on the insects. To crown all of this irritation, one was under permanent attack from swarms of mosquitoes. Nights in Pahang could be very dark indeed. I would call it a blackout. The Malays have a beautiful love song called 'Terang Bulan' (Bright Moon). This love song could well have been called the Malay national anthem. However, a bright moon seldom shone over the deep dark jungle of central Pahang!

Very little English was spoken during the day and there was no company whatsoever during the evenings apart from dinner with Middleton and Betty Lou on a Saturday night. I was completely cut off from the outside world, bored and homesick, it was beginning to get me down. I was on the verge of resigning when the Malayan Emergency broke out. This changed everything, life once again became exciting, adventurous and daring. My mode of transport around the plantation had been an old bicycle, now I was given an armoured jeep!

In September 1949, with great pleasure, I was transferred to Elmina Estate, taking over the oil palm division under Norman

Alexander, the manager. Elmina Estate was some 15 miles from Kuala Lumpur where I would meet up with other planters on a regular basis. Although the threat of bandit ambush was always present, life in general was happy and carefree. When I received my bonus for the year 1949 I bought an MG Sports Tourer (1948 model). This was indeed a lovely looking car but its performance was deeply disappointing. When it caught fire I traded it in for a new 500 cc Fiat.

The good life for me was coming to an end… I was promoted to senior assistant and posted to the 'Back Division' at Elmina – 2200 acres of rubber, some of which was in the process of being reclaimed, an arduous task for all involved. It had been left uncultivated during the Japanese occupation in WW2. Jungle plants had taken over – rhododendron, wild orchids and such like. The Back Division was well named, back it was, 'back of beyond'. To get to the back bungalow from the main road there was swamp to cross, then through the oil palm division, some 2400 acres, across another swamp and then you travelled on to the far end of the rubber division. The assistant's bungalow was situated on high ground close to the jungle's edge, which rose steeply behind it, indeed a lonely isolated spot. Because of the deep ravines, bukits and other obstacles, the dirt road to and from the bungalow had to make many detours as it wound its way to join up with the main road. With this hazardous road and continual bandit activity in the area, one could only leave the plantation when it was absolutely necessary. Once again the loneliness came back to haunt me. I reasoned that if I was to continue in the planting industry it would be necessary to find something or someone that would resolve this affliction. Without thinking of the final outcome, some single planters on lonely estates thought they had found the answer to this problem in a bottle of whisky. This shortcut did work for a time, however, the side effects could be devastating, ending up either in a mental institution or being sent home in disgrace. After considering all possible options I came to a realistic conclusion, to find a suitable 'Keep' (a kept woman), a housekeeper, a pillow dictionary, name it what you will. This was exactly what I did. Most of the European community looked down on this kind of cohabitation. They termed it 'going native'. But having decided to establish myself in the planting profession, this was the only sensible solution to the loneliness. Most of the top rubber planters in the industry found a

'Keep' to be the golden key to the loneliness during their 'Creeper' years.

I found my answer in a Malay girl called Che Puteh binti Yousaff. I first met her when I was on local leave in February 1949. Che Puteh came from Kota Bharu, a coastal town in north Kelantan close to the Siam border. She had been a 'Rongging Dancer', one of the many in Sultan of Kelantan's entertainment troupe at his Kelantan Istana. Rongging is a seductive Javanese dance.

Che Puteh was a dance hostess at the Wembley Night Club in Georgetown, Penang. In those days no European girl went to a nightclub like the Wembley, if they did, it was always with a male partner.

For most men and women alike in my era, the forties and fifties, dancing was an integral part of our social lives and at 23 I was no exception, I loved every minute of it and all types – be it country or modern. Clubs like the Wembley were a godsend. It was recommended to me by Harry Templeton, the proprietor of the Mount Pleasure Hotel at Batu Ferringgi, a few miles north of Georgetown. It was here I first met Che Puteh, a beautiful 21-year-old Malay girl. The club had an entry charge, the tariff depended on the location of your table. The nearer the dance floor, the dearer the tariff. A dance hostess could be booked out for the evening and they would stay at your table for the whole evening. A book of dance tickets could be bought allowing one to dance with any of the dance hostesses, sitting in the area around the dance band. By placing one dance ticket under her handbag next to her, one booked a dance. Drinks were all table service only, very simple Chinese meals were also served. Their speciality was baked crab in its shell, served with delicious savoury toast. Mamee, a Chinese Malayan dish was also very good. On my first night out in Georgetown, I went to the Wembley as recommended, and had several 'taxi' dances with Che Puteh. She was indeed a good dancer and I enjoyed dancing with her. The following evening I booked Che Puteh out for the entire evening and she joined me at my table. With Che Puteh's poor English and my poor Malay, communication was a little difficult at first, however we did manage to converse. She had been brought up in the Istana Court where she had been coached in Malay culture, such as, dress, gait, dance and the art of love, known as 'Kemut Berahi'. Che Puteh had a four-year-old son who was looked after by her family in Kelantan. The boy was supported by Istana Finance. She was permitted to visit her son only

41

on special occasions. She never did tell me who his father was. For several reasons, I was never sure that Che Puteh binti Youseff was her true name. But this was the name on her Emergency ID card.

Now that the ravages of time have wrecked this human frame and have taken away all my passion and the desires which I can no longer fulfil, I feel free to think and write about girls I have met and loved, especially Che Puteh. The reason for this deep recall of past love after all the passion has gone, I know not, but illogical thoughts go deep and can be relived on paper.

We danced all night long, it was like a breath of fresh air, and after a Malayan special Chinese Mamee, Che Puteh returned to Mount Pleasure Hotel with me. After a swim in the moonlit pool, we retired to the chalet where a bond of love and friendship was made. In the morning she went back to Georgetown, we arranged to meet at the Wembley that evening. As fate would have it, shortly after lunch I fell ill with what was known then as ST Malaria. This strain of Malaria is usually fatal, any survivors are immune to Malaria ever after – so far I can vouch for this fact! I took to bed and Harry Templeton phoned the Wembley to let Che Puteh know that I would not be there that evening. The next day I was due to join the charismatic, infamous Gus Molden for a curry tiffin. (During the time I knew Gus, events unfolded that are unrelated to my relationship with Che Puteh and require a detailed account of their own, which I will recount later.)

Che Puteh arrived that morning and insisted on bathing my feet. Malays (in my time) believed that all feverous germs leave the body through the feet, and bathing the feet helps to expel the germs faster. Gus Molden arrived and promptly sent for two doctors to attend me. I was put on a course of quinine. Che Puteh spent the night bathing my feet and nursing me until my fever broke. Gus gave me two weeks' convalescence leave in addition to my gratuity leave, asking the doctor to confirm this with Jim Robertson, the new manger at Sungai Tekal. After a few days the Malaria had eased. I was feeling a lot better. I took one week's leave, spending most of the time with Che Puteh. I bid her farewell in early March and did not see her again until September when I took a few days' leave before being transferred to the oil palm division on Elmina Estate. It was a great pleasure seeing her again and being close to her filled me with contentment. I told her I was now billeted on Elmina Estate, some 15 miles from Kuala Lumpur. Che Puteh decided to ask for a transfer to the Bukit Bintang (Star Hill Night Club) in

Kuala Lumpur which was part of the Wembley Night Club company, so that we could see more of each other. When I was promoted to senior assistant and took over the 'Back Division', I asked Che Puteh if she would like to come and stay with me. It was too dangerous now for me to visit Kuala Lumpur. She came to Elmina and became my housekeeper and companion. She also came with me to Ulu Buloh, Sungai Rawang, Telok Gong and Sungai Tekal Estates. Che Puteh was with me on Elmina Estate during the time of the Thomson tragedy. Whilst at Sungai Tekal, Che Puteh came through all the skirmishes and attacks made by the bandits, which were frequent during our four-year stay.

We both knew that our affair would end one day as Che Puteh always wanted to go back to Kalantan and her own culture. When I returned to Malaya from my home leave in 1955–56, it was no surprise to her when I told her what had happened back home, our parting had been inevitable. We met during troubled times, in a different world, we would never forget each other.

Che Puteh had been sterilised by a Malay bomah (native doctor) after her son was born so she could not bear any more children. This was her main reason why our affair could not last. At one stage of our relationship she offered to bring a young Malay girl into our affair so that we could have a child. But this was not an arrangement I wanted and no more was said.

Kelantan women were renowned for their feminine charm, alluring gait, elegant posture and for the way they wore their high split colourful sarongs. Che Puteh was no exception, having been trained in this manner as part of her pleasing Malay etiquette. While she was with me she taught me not only the language but many Malay customs, superstitions, sorcery charms and much more. Perhaps I had 'Gone Native'. Did Che Puteh save my life when I went down with deadly ST Malaria by administering her old Malay remedies? I like to think so.

CHAPTER 7

Abang Darah
(Blood Brothers)

On the second day of my leave from Sungai Tekal in 1949 (after the bandit attack), I was sitting having a beer with Harry at the Mount Pleasure Hotel when Gus Molden walked in with a beautiful Chinese girl. I'd first met Gus two weeks before. He was the managing director of Cumberbatch, a large agency house in K.L. in charge of Scottish Malayan, Strathmore Rubber and many other estates. Harry also knew Gus so we joined him and his girlfriend for a beer. Gus invited me for a curry tiffin he had arranged for the coming Sunday. However, that was the night I went down with a severe bout of ST malaria and was unable to get up the next day. As previously explained, Gus made arrangements for me when I was ill. He was No.1 as far as Scottish Malayan was concerned and indeed was very well liked by the locals and British alike. It was very odd meeting him in Penang, as the day prior to my leave I'd had a serious problem to discuss with him and was summoned to his office in Kuala Lumpur. I was in trouble with the Mentakab police and was about to be charged with assault on two Malays. Two weeks prior to this first meeting, when on business in Mentakab, I happened upon one of the Malay Special Police who had deserted at the time of the attack on Sungai Tekal. When I arrested him his brother came at me with a parong (large knife), so I hit him with the butt of my shotgun. The police arrived on the scene and we were taken down to the police station. Unbeknown to me, an arrangement had been reached between the Sultans of Malaya and the British government. Each state had its own Sultan, who, although he 'ruled', had to answer to the British. Any Malay bandits who surrendered and denounced communism were to be given a free pardon. At this time the ruling did not extend to Chinese bandits but subsequently they were also included in this agreement. Under this new ruling, all the Malay police who had deserted during the attack on Sungai Tekal were given a free pardon by the Sultan of

Pahang. That is how delicate the political situation was. However Gus Molden telephoned the Chief of Police and the charge of assault was dropped. How quickly an influential character can resolve a tricky situation!

I was feeling a lot better and decided to give my manager Jim Robertson a ring. He told me that he had received a letter from the doctor explaining my illness. I reassured him I was recovering and explained what a help Gus Molden had been. To my astonishment, he told me to get in touch with the police should I see Gus again. Seemingly, he had embezzled $91,000 of Scottish Malayan money! This was proceeds from the sale of oil palm and rubber from Sungai Tekal Estate earned during the period the crops were being processed by another estate. I was relieved I had not known of this before. I took one week's convalescence leave and returned to Sungai Tekal.

Two weeks later Gus was caught in Singapore trying to board ship for Australia. He was tried and given a three-year jail sentence. At his trial it came to light that in 1934 he was found guilty of embezzlement in Singapore also in 1936 in Buenos Aires. He was a qualified Chartered Accountant and during the war a colonel in the Indian Army Intelligence Service, responsible for withdrawing the Japanese currency in Malaya and replacing it with Malayan dollars. On his release from prison he took up a rubber planting billet with a Chinese company. I heard that one day the Chinese owner had followed one of his own lorries loaded with rubber and when it was stopped by police at a road block, the Chinese owner got out of his car and asked the lorry driver where he was going. The destination given by the driver was unknown to the owner! I don't know if Gus was up to his usual tricks! One will never know. Subsequently, Gus was invited to a Chinese dinner in Singapore by this boss. The next day Gus's body was found hanging in a Chinese cemetery! A belief held at the time by the Chinese was that if you were killed in a cemetery, your ghost would be held within the walls of that cemetery and would not haunt whoever did the killing or his associates. I was very sad to hear about Gus, he had been a good friend, showing concern for me when I was ill.

Shortly after Robertson took over Sungai Tekal, one of the worst incidents suffered by the security forces occurred in the area – seven policemen were killed and 20 wounded. A party of police were on their way to open a new remote jungle fort when they were ambushed. Among the bandits was another notorious Malay bandit

45

leader 'Hashim'. His wife was said to never leave his side. It was believed she always carried two hand grenades in her sarong. Hashim was worth $10,000 to the police 'dead or alive'. His wife's arrest was worth $5,000. Ironically, Hunter and Robertson were in the Malayan jungle during the war with Force 136 training the same communists in jungle warfare who were now behind all the killings and devastation.

The Pahang kampong Malays were very superstitious in those days and had some peculiar beliefs. In many ways, their way of thinking reminded me of local folklore in my home town of Kirrie. My own grandfather was very superstitious – for instance, would never have lilac flowers in the house, seeing them as harbingers of bad luck. With many Malay people I knew at the time, often seemingly ordinary events would take on a spiritual slant. I believe it is human nature to take on the beliefs, customs and culture of those you are surrounded by and I came to respect their way of thinking. By the time I left Malaya their ways had been weaved into my own character. One incident I recall, is when they called me 'blood brother' owing to the fact, some of my blood, be it minute, was in their drinking water. This phenomenon came about in a strange way in the early days of the Emergency.

The water supply to the manager's bungalow was rain collected from the roof which fed into a large storage tank at the rear of the bungalow. Every morning water was pumped by hand from the storage tank to the header tank, which in turn supplied water for the bathrooms, toilets and kitchen. As it rained most afternoons around 4 p.m. there was an ample supply of water, under normal conditions. However, with the outbreak of the Emergency and with a section of twelve Special Police stationed at the bungalow, day and night, another source of water had to be found. The bungalow stood on a bukit (hill) at the foot of which was an old disused well, built before WW2 with jungle timbers. This supply of water was the answer to the problem. Attached to the well was an old hand pump in need of repair. When the Chinese fitter tried to remove the pump from the well the suction pipe was jammed at the bottom and would not budge. I dived in to have a look and found one of the old cross support timbers had fallen on the suction non-return valve, so I removed it and took the pump out of the well. When I surfaced, the water in the well was blood red. I hadn't realised that during the dive my head had struck a protruding rusty nail on one of the cross supports, the gash was some two inches in length and pouring blood. The estate dresser sealed the wound with eight stitches. The scar is with me to this day. The Chinese fitter repaired the pump and water was pumped to the storage tank at the bungalow. The water remained a reddish colour for several days, probably due to rust from the pipes, but from then on the Malayan police at the bungalow considered themselves to be my darah dan daging (flesh and blood) 'blood brothers'. They were strongly advised to boil all their drinking water hereafter! After the water tank incident I was jokingly referred to as a 'blood brother', but it seemed to stick. I have often wondered if this was the reason the Malay police at the bungalow, after this event, remained loyal when the estate was attacked.

The Luger Mystery

On 10th November 1949, a band of Malayan bandits gave themselves up at kampong Sebak near Kuala Krau. Among them were a large number of former Special Police who had deserted and joined the bandits the previous year, following the attack on Sungai Tekal. They were the men that Middleton and I had enlisted to guard the estate when the Emergency broke out. There is one event that happened on Sungai Tekal, which to this day has not been solved. The mystery of Luger Pistol No. 942. In December 1948, I bought the Luger Pistol from our visiting medical officer on his retirement. I then sold it on to a Sergeant Dave Griffith, one of the reinforcements sent to Sungai Tekal. This Luger caused endless trouble involving the Malayan, London and Rhodesian CID. I had left the gun's transfer papers with Sergeant Griffith to complete. He then went back to England before taking up a position with the South Rhodesian Police in Bulawayo. However, the transfer was not recorded and, after a lot of barter, the CID was called in to solve the problem. The matter has never been resolved. To this day Luger 942 is still registered in my name on the Malayan Licence to possess arms certificate. I often wonder where this Luger is today. No doubt it has quite a history! The date on the Luger was 1913 with initials engraved in silver on the stock, probably a first world war German officer.

Angus Ogilvy

Among the many regiments on active service in Malaya during the emergency was the Scots Guards and one of its serving officers was Captain Angus Ogilvy. He was the son of the Earl of Airlie and heir to the Airlie Estate at Cortachy by Kirriemuir, Angus.

Seemingly Jock Hunter the founder of Scottish Malayan Estates and the Strathmore Rubber Company was a son of a farmer on the Airlie Estate. The first plantation that Hunter cut out of the Malayan jungle and planted with rubber trees he named Strathairlie Estate.

The son of the founder was Mac Hunter and on hearing that Angus Ogilvy was in Malaya and stationed near Kuala Lumpur, invited Angus to Strathairlie for a curry tiffin (Mac Hunter was managing Director of Scottish Malayan Estates) followed by a punai (pigeon) shoot over the swamp on Elmina Estate six miles from Strathairlie, where Norman Alexander had arranged for a cocktail party after the shoot.

Every evening just before sunset between 6 and 7pm thousands of punai would fly low over the swamp from their feeding grounds to roost in the tall jungle trees close by. The estate road crossed the swamp which was an ideal spot for the shooters to stand and wait for the incoming punai. Being the first shoot of the season, it was good and with nine guns the kill was in the region of some 150 birds, most of which were given to Angus to be served up in the Officer's Mess. The punai is a small pigeon and was considered a delicacy by planters. My Chinese cook's speciality was pigeon on toast served with a delicious spicy sauce.

The cocktail party went on well into the night and in conversation Angus mentioned that he was thinking of visiting some friends in Port Dickson and Singapore as soon as he could arrange transport and asked Norman if he could borrow his armoured plated Ford Mercury with his Malay Sais (chauffeur). He was offered use of the car and made plans to visit Singapore. That night Angus left Elmina Estate in the chauffeur driven armoured car for his billet in Kuala Lumpur. He kept the car for five days and made no attempt to contact Elmina Estate. The Sais drove him and a fellow Officer all round Singapore, waiting for them every night while they dined out. He was never offered cash or food, and no arrangements were made for his accommodation and they even expected him to pay for the petrol. When the Sais returned to Elmina, Norman was told what had happened and was very upset, so he wrote to Ogilvy demanding an explanation regarding the appalling way the Malay sais was treated. Norman told me he never received a reply.

While on the subject of Angus Ogilvy and the Scots Guards there is an incident which remains to haunt the Battalion. Newspapers at the time reported on the event and there were various rumours about what had really happened.

On 11th December 1948 a fourteen man patrol from the Scots Gurads were searching for CT in the jungle near Kampong Batang Kali north of Kuala Lumpur, they came across a small squatter settlement of Chinese rubber tappers working on a plantation. The patrol suspected the Chinese squatters of supplying food to CT guerrillas and separated the men from the women. The men were held in a kongsi hut overnight and interrogated. In the early hours of the morning there was confusion outside the kongsi, it was reported that the Scots Guards thought the squatters were about to escape and called them to halt, then acting on orders opened fire, killing twenty five of the squatters leaving non wounded or injured. The Scots Guards were only in Malaya for a few weeks and for some of the men it was their first patrol. There was no officer and a Lance Sergeant was in charge, the Sergeant had no transport, no radio, no means of communication with his officer. The so called Batang Kali "secret massacre" caused an outcry in Malaya and the U.K. Inquiries went on until 1970 without a conclusion. The charges surfaced again in a 1993 BBC documentary "In Cold Blood".

CHAPTER 8

The Thomson Tragedy

It was September 1949, I was transferred to Elmina Estate, Sungai Buloh Selangor, a large oil palm and rubber estate some eighteen miles from Kuala Lumpur. The estate was managed by Norman Alexander an SME senior planter. My duties were to manage the oil palm division. I stayed with Joe Walker, the rubber division manager, for the first four weeks until repairs to the assistant's bungalow were finished, it having been left vacant during the Japanese occupation.

The first day I moved into the bungalow I went into the bathroom and was about to sit on the loo when I noticed the large head of an iguana lizard with gaping jaws looking up at me from the toilet pan. If I had sat down without looking? Disaster! I went to fetch a stick from the kitchen but when the cook and I got back to the bathroom the lizard had gone. We then inspected the septic tank and found a colony of iguana lizards living there. The concrete walls of the tank were clean and white as snow. As the tank had been out of use for a few years after the Japanese occupation, the bacteria had had time to completely dissolve any trace of waste. The Tamil cook and gardener had a field day – curried iguana was a delicacy with the Tamil Indians. I politely declined to share in their good fortune!

I spent six months looking after the oil palm division, after which I was promoted to Senior Assistant and put in charge of the rubber division, Joe Walker having been promoted to Manager of Sungai Tekal Estate. The rubber division was known as the 'Back division' 2200 acres in all, with its own factory and labour force. It was called 'back division' because it was some six miles from the main government road. The assistant's bungalow was on a high piece of land close to the jungle edge, which rose steeply behind it. An isolated and lonely place. The bungalow guard consisted of ten Malay Special Police and a corporal. There was no telephone or wireless link with the main office so communications with the office was done by a Tamil messenger on a cycle. My method of transport was an old army BSA motorcycle. My manager, Norman Alexander, visited once or twice a week; I also met him, from time to time, when it was necessary for me to go to the main office. My old oil palm division was handed to Sandy Murray, a new assistant. Sandy had just arrived in Malaya, he was from Aberdeen. The ongoing communist trouble was relentless. Frequent ambushes, rubber tree slashing and intimidation of the labour force, all had to be endured.

The saddest and most tragic event I ever witnessed happened on Saturday 25th November 1950. Bob Thomson (Bob had taken over from Norman Alexander the previous month) and his wife Dorothy had invited Sandy Murray and myself to join them for dinner at the Selangor Club in Kuala Lumpur to celebrate St Andrew's Day. On the morning of that day Bob and Dorothy, along with a full police escort, left early. Bob went to visit another rubber estate a few miles south of Kuala Lumpur. On the way he dropped off Dorothy in Kuala Lumpur to visit a friend. Before leaving, Bob asked me to inspect his bungalow's police guard and to check with the ayah (children's nanny) if Susan, his three-year-old daughter was safe and sound before leaving to join them for dinner.

The Thomsons' bungalow staff consisted of Susan's ayah (with her own two young children), cook, houseboy, sais and gardener; there was also a Malay police guard of one corporal and twelve Malay Special Police on duty during the hours of darkness. Later that morning the police Lieutenant in charge of all special police in the district arrived to inspect the police guard. After the inspection he stayed for lunch, he was also going to the St Andrew's celebrations. He suggested I bring my dress suit and come across to his bungalow for afternoon tea. As his residence was closer to the Thomsons' bungalow I took up his offer.

The Elmina Estate road crossed a swamp, a distance of almost half a mile, where it joined the government road. At the junction there was a Chinese shop and café where the local bus from Kuala Lumpur stopped. Thomson had arranged with the bus company to have the daily paper dropped off at the café. The Thomsons' houseboy would cycle across the swamp every afternoon at 4 p.m. to collect the papers.

The Lieutenant's bungalow was some 400 yards from the café. During our afternoon tea, we were startled by several bursts of machine gunfire, which we thought came from behind the café. A Sergeant and eight police were sent to investigate. They found nothing out of place and were told the firing came from somewhere in the swamp. We then received a phone call from Sandy Murray to say the estate Land Rover had been ambushed in the swamp and that Susan Thomson and Madasamy (the houseboy) had both been killed.

The Lieutenant and I dashed across to the scene where we found the Land Rover lying on its side in the swamp. This was a horrible tragedy. As the Thomsons were away, the bungalow staff thought it a good idea to go and collect the papers from the café in the Land Rover. The ayah decided to go as well, taking Susan and her own two young children along for the ride. The bandits had laid an ambush on a mount in the swamp, close to the estate road. The Land Rover driver said the bandits had not waited to see what happened and made a quick getaway. When we approached the car we could see Susan had been killed outright, the back of her tiny head blown off. Muthasammy had been shot through the heart and the driver was wounded in the leg and arm. The ayah and her two children escaped with minor bruises.

Sandy Murray alerted all the services. Susan, Muthasammy and the driver were taken to the general hospital in Kuala Lumpur. Sandy and I left immediately for Kuala Lumpur to find Bob and Dorothy. We then had the awful task of telling them about the horrific tragedy. At first they would not believe it and could not accept what had happened. The funerals were arranged for the next day. When I spoke to Bob in the morning he asked me to go up to the hospital and arrange for the burial of Muthasammy his loyal 'houseboy' (a name I never liked) who had been with him for several years before the war.

Sandy and I bought some flowers and went to the hospital morgue. Muthasammy was lying on a slab in the same clothes he was killed in. Next to him was a young Chinese girl, about five years old, she was just skin and bone, coming out of her nose was a large tape worm with another coming out of her ear, (probably caused by eating undercooked wild pork). I asked the attendant if he could cover her up. With a look of disdain, he doubled the child up and squeezed her into a tiny soap box. At this point I lost my temper and threw him out of the room. When things had calmed down, a tipper lorry arrived. Our Muthasammy was put on the lorry along with the young Chinese girl and others. We followed the lorry to the People's Cemetery where a bulldozer was waiting, having dug a large hole. The lorry carrying the dead backed up and tipped all the bodies into the hole. I said a small prayer and we threw the flowers into the hole. The bulldozer went to work filling in the hole. Sandy and I were the only mourners there. I left the People's Cemetery with a sore heart.

Report of Thomson Ambush November 1950

That afternoon we went to the funeral parlour where Susan had been taken before her burial. Here we found a very different scene. Susan lay in a beautiful white coffin with all due care and respect being given to her. She was slowly taken to the European Cemetery and laid to rest. Sad as the two deaths were, the difference haunts me to this day. This was British Malaya 1950. I look back on that sad event with conflicting thoughts.

In April of that year the 8th Battalion of The Malayan People's Anti-British Army attacked the Chinese village of Kepong some six miles from the Elmina estate. During the attack seventeen police were killed. However, the communists withdrew when their commander, the 30-year-old Chan Sam Yin, was killed – he was shot in the back by a Chinese auxiliary policeman. There had been a $20,000 reward for his death or capture. During WW2 Chan had been a member of 136 Force. It was a platoon from the 8th Battalion that attacked the Land Rover in which Susan Thomson and Muthasammy were killed.

After the tragedy of their daughter's death, Bob and Dorothy were given an extended home leave and Pat Stewart took over Management of the estate.

Pat Stewart

Pat Stewart came from Coupar in Fife. Shortly after he took over Elmina Estate, his wife Mabel left with their two children and went back to Scotland. Pat had one major problem – he drank! Consequently his work suffered and office management was left undone due to his drinking. I had engaged a new Chinese rubber tapping contractor with 150 tappers. Their new contracts needed Pat's signature. I had asked him on several occasions for this, as the Chinese contractor would not go ahead without a written agreement. The contractor and myself went to Pat's bungalow and were let in by one of his staff. Pat was still in bed, I woke him up and asked him to sign the contract. He got up and came through to the lounge, sat down and called to his houseboy in Malay to bring him some water. The houseboy asked if I wanted any, I asked for water and orange. Pat drank his down in one go. I took a sip of mine and spat it straight out. It was neat gin! Seemingly Pat had an arrangement with his staff to bring him gin whenever he asked for water, in order to fool his wife.

The company retired Pat on medical grounds (beriberi). Pat, like many senior planters in Scottish Malayan, had been a prisoner of the Japanese during the war and had gone through hell on the Burma Railway. When Pat got back home he was still drinking heavily and had lost nearly everything. At times he worked as a part-time clerk in the Sugar Beet factory at Coupar, Fife. Then, out of the blue, he was left the Park Hotel in St Andrews by an aunt. We all thought that would be the end of Pat Stewart and drink would kill him. Some twenty years later I was in the canning business, a farmer in Fife, Marshall Forrester, was growing strawberries on contract for me. On one visit to his farm he showed me a French shotgun which he had just purchased. I told him I had seen a similar one belonging to a rubber planter in Malaya. 'Was it Pat Stewart?' he asked. It turned out that Pat and Marshall were friends and this was the same gun.

After taking over the hotel, Pat became teetotal and had joined Alcoholics Anonymous. I asked Marshall to give Pat my regards. That evening I received a call from Marshall telling me that Pat wanted to see me as soon as possible. We arranged to meet for lunch the following week at his hotel in St Andrews.

When I arrived there the following week, I asked for Pat at reception, just at that moment he came down the stairs carrying two suitcases. Unbelievably, he looked younger than the last time I had seen him twenty years previously, when saying goodbye at Port Swettenham. He now passed me by without any sign of recognition. When I said "Good Morning," he put down the cases and shaking my hand briskly, cried out "Dykes Aitkenhead!" During lunch with him and his wife, he explained, that although I had been his assistant for nearly a year, he never knew what I looked like, but when I spoke, he recognised me by my voice alone. That was all he could remember from his dark drinking days.

Bill Allen's Accident

While on the subject of Elmina Estate there is another sorrowful tale to tell. This tragedy took place in the assistant's bungalow on the oil palm division in late 1952. Two weeks before going home on six months' leave I met the new assistant Bill Allen who was from Forfar, five miles from my hometown of Kirriemuir. Bill asked me to look up his girlfriend when I got home and this I did on two occasions. At the last meeting she gave me a present to take back to Bill. Inconceivably, three days after I saw him and delivered the present, Bill was dead! He and Jim Alexander, who was due to go on home leave, were sitting on the veranda one evening, having a beer, when Jim decided to clean his carbine rifle, before handing it back to the Sungai Buloh Police. As he was cleaning it, the gun accidentally went off shooting Bill through the heart! Jim was charged with manslaughter. At the inquest it was revealed that Bill was in fact married to his girlfriend. To become an assistant with Scottish Malayan you had to be single and remain single during your first five-year agreement. Bill was single at the time of his interview but he married before sailing to Malaya and kept it a secret. Scottish Malayan had their assistants insured for £20,000 and their managers for £40,000 on death. They paid out £40,000 to Bill's widow, a lot of money in those days.

Jim was given a suspended jail sentence and sailed home as booked. During his home leave he was in a shockingly nervous state, however, he summoned up the courage to visit Bill Allen's girlfriend. Strange as it may sound, several years later they were married.

John McGregor's wife Ella

In January 1951 I was transferred to Sungai Buloh Estate, owned by the Strathmore Rubber Company, as assistant to the managing director Mac Hunter, son of the founder Jock Hunter. Sungai Buloh (Bamboo River) was one of the first plantations that Jock cut out of the jungle and planted with rubber trees. 1500 acres of Sungai Buloh was in the process of being replanted with a high yielding clone of rubber trees. In addition there was an experimental five-acre plot of cocoa. I enjoyed working with Mac, he was very positive and all matters were dealt with smoothly. His positive attitude made the task in hand much easier.

During this time he and his wife Joyce went home on their six-month leave and I took over Strathairlie, the other estate Mac managed. John McGregor took over as acting general manager. One of his duties was to visit all the estates and write up a monthly report on each and send them to the directors in Edinburgh. On one of McGregor's visits, the itinerary was 6 a.m. at Riverside Estate, an estate managed by Jimmy Baxter; 11 a.m. at Strathairlie where I was to meet him; 2 p.m. at Elmina Estate where his wife Ella was to join him for a late lunch. A good day's work in all with a lot to see to.

After waiting at Strathairlie office for some three hours I received a telephone call from Ella asking for John's whereabouts as it was now after 2 p.m. The only information I had, was that John and Jimmy Baxter had left Riverside at about 11 a.m. I passed this on to Ella, who was not best pleased! Shortly after, McGregor's armour-plated American Ford Mercury V8 pulled up outside. The Malay sais winked at me and I knew something was up. John and Jimmy got out of the car and I was very well met. I could smell the alcohol! The inspection was called off! They were going to Kuala Lumpur and wanted me to join them, which I did. John was told that Ella was anxious about him, however he told the office clerk to telephone her to say he was okay.

We set off for Kuala Lumpur. The first port of call was the Coliseum Bar in Batu Road, a planter's meeting place. We stayed there a few hours, did the usual rounds ending up in the Hong Tock Hotel in the Kepong road. Whilst sitting drinking and joking with a few 'ladies' of the hotel, Ella McGregor walked in, picked up a bottle from the table and hit John over the head, threatened both myself and Jimmy with it and chased the ladies from the bar. She then wrecked the place, walked out and drove off at top speed. John was on the floor bleeding badly from a head wound. We took him to the general hospital where he had eight stitches. In the Hong Tock from then on we were known as the 'orange gila' (mad people) by the staff and 'ladies'. It was some ten days later before John got round to finishing his visiting reports. During WW2, Ella had driven through a Japanese check point with a truck full of Europeans escaping the occupation. They were fired on but escaped unharmed through the border crossing. You didn't mess with Ella!

CHAPTER 9

The Crocodile and New Assistants

In August 1951 I was promoted to Manager and took over Sungai Rawang Estate (River Gap), an oil palm plantation at Tanong Sepat and Bedford Estate, a rubber plantation at Batu Laut on the coast road going north from Port Dickson towards Klang. Sungai Rawang Estate had a unique network of canals for transporting, after harvest, fruit bunches, in barges, to the oil palm factory. In October of that year, Telok Gong Estate was added to my workload, when Arthur Grant the manager went home on long leave. In view of this, I was given two assistants to ease the load. However in the first few months it made things more difficult as they were fresh out from Scotland and posted straight to me at the height of the Emergency.

Jock Marchant, a farmer's son from Laurencekirk, was the first to arrive. He stayed with me for two weeks on Sungai Rawang prior to moving on to Telok Gong Estate. This helped him, as it gave him some idea of the workings of an oil palm plantation. When Mike Turner arrived it was different matter. He only spent two days with me on Telok Gong and that was all. The company had insisted he go straight to Bedford Estate as the labour force there was unsettled as they did not have a permanent manager. This was far too swift a culture change! Bedford Estate was approximately a quarter of a mile from the main coast road and the assistant's bungalow was in a fairly isolated position. Firstly, the estate would be a vulnerable target for the bandits, having no police stationed there. Also the only person on the estate who could speak English was an Indian conductor (dresser/clerk/nurse) who was responsible for the daily running of the estate. Without a resident manager things could get out of hand, such as payroll inconsistencies, false rice and milk accounts. The communists would raid the rice stores and mix freely with the labour force. In view of this the authorities were on the verge of closing the plantation down, therefore it was necessary for a manger to be in residence with a company of Special Police. We recruited a police force, managing to find two Malays who could speak a little English, which did help. However, this was not the ideal situation for a young man fresh out from Scotland. Turner was small, slim and understandably nervous.

The first night he spent alone in the bungalow the telephone wires were cut and a few shots were fired by the bandits. The next morning I made Bedford Estate my first call. I found Tuner had repacked and was in the process of making arrangements for his passage home, the special police having repaired the cut telephone wires. To persuade him to stay, I told him that Jock Marchant and myself would stay with him for a few weeks until he felt more settled. He finally agreed to this and Jock moved in that night. Sungai Rawang was only a few miles down the coast road and Marchant had done his National Service in the RAF, as had Turner, so they had something in common. Marchant was the perfect companion for Turner, having a robust attitude with a good sense of humour. Turner did eventually settle in, but only just; he left the company the following year.

Killing the Crocodile

In October 1951 I moved to Telok Gong Estate which was situated some twelve miles south of Klang on the Sungai Langat (River Langal). It was almost an island, the river being round three quarters of the plantation. In this area the river was called Sungai Buaya (crocodile river) by the local Malays – well named!

The estate labour force was Tamil and one of their pastimes was crocodile hunting, mainly for food – the meat was considered a delicacy. There were two methods of hunting: one by snaring, the other, a little more gruesome – a dog or goat would be killed, gutted and a piece of jungle timber of about five inches in diameter stitched inside the carcass with a rope attached to it. The carcass was then cast into the river and the rope tied to a tree. The crocodile would bite into the carcass, its bite being so powerful that it would get so firmly embedded in the timber sealed within the carcass that it could not let go. The crocodile was then pulled to the river bank, hit on the head to kill it and gutted immediately, a messy operation all round! Seemingly, the expansion muscle of a crocodile's jaw is calculated at 3lbs in strength and the closing contraction muscle has a strength of 300lbs, quite a bite, and that is how it works, so I've been told.

The rubber factory and office were situated down by the river and there was an old jetty from which, in pre-war days, rubber was loaded onto barges and taken down river to Port Swettenham, some 15 miles to the north. The office overlooked the river which at this point was approximately 120 yards wide. From my desk there was an excellent view of the opposite bank. Most of the time crocodiles would be lying asleep along this sandy bank with birds picking leeches from their bodies. Crocodiles were of particular danger when working close to the river. Even at this distance from the sea the river was still slightly tidal, which made it more dangerous. One had to be careful. Occasionally a Tamil or Chinese worker would be attacked by a crocodile, and women washing clothes were an easy quarry. I could never understand why they did their washing down at the river. They were all well aware of the dangers. During my short stay on Telok Gong a Tamil women from the labour force disappeared, she was last seen at the river's edge washing clothes.

One afternoon in late January 1952, while sitting at my desk in the office down on the old river wharf, a huge crocodile came out of the river and lay in the sun on the sandy bank opposite. It was massive compared to the rest, it could have been 12 feet or more. I decided to kill it there and then. Ali, one of the Malay Police escorts, asked the police corporal to bring to the office as many Malay police as he could muster. This prize would be a meal for the Tamil labour force and some extra cash for myself, to spend on home leave (which was now overdue). The corporal arrived with six men and with the escort made a firing squad of ten riffles.

It was explained to the corporal that we were to kill the crocodile. He ordered his men to lie down on the bank, aim carefully for the crocodile's head and fire on the command of three. This was duly done but the bullets hit the trees, the water, the sandbank and the bushes, a terrific volley hitting everything but the crocodile. The reptile rose and made for the water and swam towards us. The noise of the gunfire had cleared the banks of all the crocodiles. They had now entered the river!

At the time, I was carrying an automatic 12 bore shotgun loaded with five rounds of large grape (buckshot). As the crocodile swam closer, I fired the five rounds at its head. There was a lot of blood, then the crocodile dived and disappeared from sight.

The evening following the crocodile shoot, the poor shooting was discussed. The corporal explained the reason for the missed shots. First he asked me if I had ever known of a Malay being taken by a crocodile? I hadn't. The reason he gave was, once a year the Malays, living in the kampongs along the Sungai Langat (river sky), hold a Hari Raya Buaya (crocodile festival). On that day the crocodiles are fed, flowers cast on the river and no fishing takes place. The local Malays believed, if the crocodiles are left alone they will leave you alone. A ritual they believed worked, which I respected and upheld from then on. However, some two months later, just before my departure for home leave, it was rumoured that a young Malay girl had been taken by a crocodile. That evening I spoke to the corporal about it and he confirmed it to be true. The corporal explained that it was a Jahat (wicked/evil) crocodile that had taken the girl and that the kampong bomah/pawang (witchdoctor), would charm it out of the river and kill it. The Pawang had been working on it for the past week, day and night, without success. This I had to see. The following afternoon I made a visit to the kampong and sure enough there was the Pawang, all in white, sitting by the river's edge, playing a small odd-shaped drum. He truly had been sitting there for the past week, playing this weird looking drum.

Two days later the corporal reported that the Jahat (crocodile) was dead, the Pawang had done his job and the dead crocodile was there for all to see!

That afternoon I went back to the kampong and sure enough, there was the crocodile with its stomach cut open. There were several scars on its head and I was told it was blind. When I asked the kampong datoh (village chief) how they knew that this was the same crocodile that took away the girl, his answer was brief – the pawang had found the gelang (anklet) the girl was wearing, in its stomach. Was this the same crocodile that I had shot? We will never know. Chinese did hunt crocodiles on this river with shotguns. One thing was certain, the crocodile had been wounded and was unable to hunt for food in the normal way. Before WW2 there had been a reward of 30cents a foot, payable in respect for crocodiles surrendered, dead or alive, to the police. I was told of a certain enterprising Chinese man on the Sungai Langat, who made a regular living in this way, until it was discovered he was breeding them in a crocodile farm upstream in the jungle.

The Danish Planter

George Stalker a Royal Marine Commando, the brother of a dear pal of mine, Jim, was posted to Malaya in late 1951 and was for sometime stationed at Seremban, a town some forty miles from

Telok Gong. George and his Irish pal John spent their first local leave here on Telok Gong. As they were coming to a rubber estate it was necessary for them to carry arms and permission for this had to be obtained from their Commanding Officer, which was duly given. The company car (Ford Mercury V8 armour-plated) together with an escort went to pick them up at Seremban as arranged. They brought with them their riffles and 100 rounds of ammunition. Being keen to find out about the manufacture of rubber and palm oil, they spent the first three days with me on the daily rounds of the three plantations and found it interesting. A few local planter friends knowing that two British soldiers were on leave here did more than enough to entertain them with offers of lunch and dinner etc. A couple of nights we went up to Klang and took part in Malay Rongging, (Malay dancing), much to Che Puteh's amusement. Close to the estate was a small Malay kampong called Momib, with a beautiful beach and small Chinese café. Most afternoons they spent swimming and learning to play Mah-jong with the local Chinese. On the last day of their leave (in camp by 2300hrs) we were invited to a curry tiffin by Vieburg, a Danish planter who was my next door neighbour when I was on Sungai Rawang. As we approached Vieburg's bungalow we were intrigued to see his previously well-manicured lawn had now disappeared! Apparently, the previous Saturday Vieburg had invited his neighbour Jock Marchant over to admire his new tractor. They were both from farming stock and after a few beers, had challenged one another to a ploughing match... They never could agree as to who had won!

The party went on well into the night, Danish style. However Vieburg's plantation was only a short distance from Seremban camp, some 20 miles away, so the boys got back to their camp on time. I did not see George again for several years. On the few occasions we do meet, the subject always reverts back to Malaya and the time he and John spent on Telok Gong in the early spring of 1952, during the height of the Emergency.

Home Leave

On 2nd April 1952 I sailed out of George Town, Penang, on six months' home leave. Before leaving Telok Gong a new 1952 Ford Consul car was purchased from Wearne Bothers, Kuala Lumpur for home delivery, to be picked up at the Ford Motor Co. showrooms, 88 Regent Street, London. From there an AA driver would drive through London to the Great North Road (A1) for a fee of 2/6 (12½p in decimal coinage). The total cost of the car taxed and fully insured was £490, including freight back to Malaya. No purchase tax was paid on the car as it was for export. Coincidentally a Mr Jack Lowden of Kirriemuir was at one time Manager at Wearne Brother, Kuala Lumpur. The voyage home was enjoyable and I arrived back in Liverpool on 27th April, which gave me the best four months possible to be on home leave. Most of the time I spent in and around Kirrie meeting old cronies. I attended Scottish Malayan Board Meetings in Edinburgh and on the second meeting was appointed manager of Sungai Tekal Estate for a period of three years.

With Granny Campbell outside her cottage, Northmuir, Kirrie (first home leave)

A passage back to Malaya was booked on the *Atreus* Blue Funnel Line, sailing out of Liverpool on 25th August '52. It carried twelve passengers. All the usual deck activities were enjoyed during the voyage, and a swimming pool was erected on deck which pleased all on board. The ship docked in Penang on 16th September and from there I made my way to Sungai Tekal by rail. During this journey I became aware that there had been no or little improvements to the rail service between Gemas and the north, since the end of the war, still the same old carriages and wooden seats, although the railhead now reached Kota Bharu, near the Siamese border. Planters like myself were mindful of the hardships endured by the POWs on the Burma railway. Their chances of survival were almost zero percent.

CHAPTER 10
The Railway of Death

During the Japanese occupation of Malaya (1942–1945) the Japanese had removed all rails and sleepers from the rail head at Gemas Junction on the Negri Sembilan/Jahore state boundary. They were used to build the notorious 'Railway of Death' into Burma. 61,000 prisoners of war were forced to work on the Siam-Burma Railway in atrocious conditions. There were additionally about 250,000 natives (coolies) who were previously residents of countries including Java, Singapore, Malaya and Burma, and many Tamil Indians who had worked in some of these countries. The railway which was 421 kms long, single track and 1M gauge, had been constructed in little over 12 months. Over this period approximately 13,000 prisoners of war died. This included 6,500 British, 2,800 Dutch and 2,700 Australians. Over the same period it is estimated that 100,000 natives died.

The railway in use at Sungai Tekal

Before I go further – A dear old pal of mine George McHardy, having been rescued from Dunkirk in 1940 was sent to the Far East. He was captured by the Japanese when Singapore fell. From there, George was sent to work on 'death railway'. Surviving this, he was then transported to Japan to mine coal. Thankfully he was underground at Hiroshima when the Americans dropped the atomic bomb. When he was finally rescued he was thin, weak and badly under-nourished, suffering from beriberi. He was sent to Canada for urgent medical care before being repatriated to Scotland. George was one of the very few lucky ones who survived this inhumane ordeal. He seldom spoke about his military service or the treatment he endured as a Japanese POW. Like myself, George enjoyed a drink, and we had many happy times together. He and his wife Reta have both passed away now and sadly missed, but the daughters in both our families are still friends to this day.

Some Scottish Malayan estate managers and assistants had also been POWs working on the railway of death, some having lived and served on Sungai Tekal. I often wondered what their thoughts were whilst dismantling the three-mile stretch of rail that runs alongside Sungai Tekal Estate.

After removing the rails and sleepers the Japanese converted the old track into a dangerous, makeshift road. Bridges were left, of which there were many, some over very high ravines. Jungle timbers were cut and made into planks and tied to the old bridge girders with bamboo straps to make road bridges. Crossing by car or lorry was a hazardous experience. Many of the rough-cut jungle timber planks had to be made secure before venturing onto the bridge. At Sungai Dalam Halt (Deep River Halt) some three miles south of the plantation there was, in particular, a dangerous high bridge over a very deep ravine – much care was needed here when crossing, the jungle timber planks moved and rattled when vehicles passed over them, the noise was unbelievable; in addition, the threat of bandit ambushes, were frequent. In those days there was very little motorised transport in this isolated part of Pahang. Most of the Malay kampongs were along the banks of the Sungai Pahang and the river was the main method of transport, there were also a few bullock carts. There were 17 bridges built with hardwood jungle timber to maintain on the Sungai Tekal Estate. This single primitive converted track was the most dangerous road I've ever travelled. This was the only road into Sungai Tekal Estate. In 1948 the British Malayan Government rebuilt the railway as far as Sungai Tekal Halt and it was completed in 1950, thus joining up with the Siamese rail network at Rantua Paniang, Kelantan.

Armoured rail vehicle used for transportation between Sungai, Tekal and Mentakab

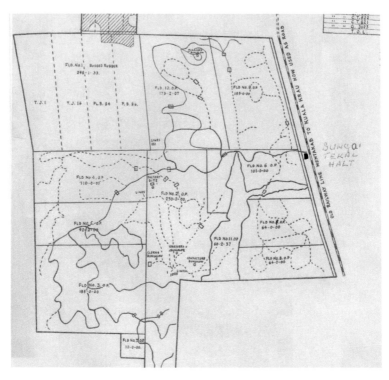

Sungai Tekal showing the railway on the east side of the estate

CHAPTER 11
Return to Sungai Tekal

On arriving back at Sungai Tekal, I realised Duncan Kidd, the manager, and his wife were very pleased to see me as they were longing for home leave. Duncan was an old acquaintance of mine. We were both assistants together down in Selangor.

As I had been billeted on Sungai Tekal before, it made the takeover easy and no problems ensued. Since my last time here there had been a big improvement in the defences of the estate. The old barbed wire fences around the factories, labour lines and bungalow compounds had been replaced with a chain link, bulldog mesh fence, with an electric generator to supply power for flood lighting around the perimeter. Because of the ambush risk the manager, Duncan, moved from the large outlying bungalow to the old manager's bungalow within the workers' compound, closer to both the oil palm and rubber factories.

The Boring Beetles

All the main beams of the old bungalow were built with round jungle timbers and it stood on stilts six feet above the ground. Every timber was riddled with holes caused by 'boring beetles', a large powerful looking insect about the size of a 50 pence piece, with a saw-like jaw that bored into the timber. The only safe way to keep the numbers down was to bang on the timbers and wait for the beetles to come out, then belt them with a tennis racket. The beetles could take off at a fair speed and had a loud buzzing sound. However time was running out for the beetles. A few months later they were all eradicated by Warrior Ants… It began one afternoon while my assistant Dodd Cables and I were having afternoon tea. A colony of ants appeared on the telephone wires, entering the bungalow just below the atop roof. They systematically killed and carried off the carcases of the beetles in bits and pieces. The battle lasted a good week. The beetles were like dive bombers trying to knock the ants off the telephone wires, but slowly bit by bit, one by one, every single beetle met its demise.

Hitting the Steamroller

The Emergency in Pahang had not improved and it was widely known that some 2,000 communist guerrillas operated in the state, 500 in and around the Mentakab area. In view of this, Mac Hunter purchased, for Sungai Tekal, an ex-army Morris armoured scout car. It weighed some 4 tons and was new with only 80 miles on the clock and would have carried a crew of five men. It was arranged that the vehicle would be picked up at Wearne Brothers, Kuala Lumpur. I flew down from Temerloh with an escort of three Malay Special Police to collect the vehicle. On our way back we stopped at Bentong for lunch. From Bentong to Mentabak the road was very lonely with many sharp bends, and on rounding one of the bends I was confronted with a steamroller. When the Malay driver saw the scout car he tried to give us more room to pass, but the back of the steamroller moved over to the centre of the road and as we passed the scout car hit one of the roller's large back wheels. There was a loud bang and we stopped. Then a Malay road worker came up to us carrying a side towing eye which had sheared off on impact saying "You have dropped this, Tuan." I thanked him for it, then asked the driver if everything was OK. He laughed and said, "OK, Tuan? I'm in a steamroller!" Before loading the car onto the flat-top rail wagon at Mentakab station, I thought it best to report the accident to the Mentakab police. The desk sergeant also laughed when a steamroller was mentioned.

When we got to Sungai Tekal Halt we were met by my assistant Dodd Cables. The flat-top rail wagon was pushed into the siding ramp and we drove off followed by Dodd in the armoured Land Rover. On arrival at the bungalow, Dodd mentioned that something was wrong with the back axel as it was out of line. We found that the eye bolts in both back springs had sheared, causing the whole axel to slide to one side of the vehicle (some impact); this was repaired, at little cost by a Chinese estate fitter.

Archie Campbell

The following week I was again driving along the Bentong road with a fellow planter Archie Campbell. He was my next door neighbour, some five miles down the railway track at Kerdau. Archie managed a large Chinese-owned rubber estate, Kerdau Plantations Ltd. Like myself, Archie was from Kirriemuir and had been with Scottish Malayan Estates between the wars. During WW1 he was a Wireless

Officer in the Merchant Navy and held the first wireless licence in Scotland, so I'm told. Before taking up a planting billet in Malaya, he opened the first wireless repair shop in Kirriemuir. His brother Peter opened the first motor repair garage in the town, which he managed until his death in 1970. At one time the Ogilvie Arms Hotel in Kirrie was the family residence. Anyway, we were going to attend a Planters' Meeting in Bentong and I had just finished telling Archie about the steamroller accident, when we approached the next bend and the steamroller appeared. On one side of the road lay its back wheel. The impact of a four-ton armoured vehicle travelling at 40 miles per hour had fractured its axel and as it moved the back wheel fell off, or something like that.

Archie Campbell standing by the vehicle I hit the steamroller with.

In early January 1953 all planters in Central Pahang were warned that there was an extremely large concentration of armed Chinese on the Siam border. These reinforcements were making their way south to join up with the 2nd Battalion of the Malayan People's Anti-British Army which was now operating in the Bentong, Mentakab and Temerloh areas of Pahang. Terrorist activity in and around the estate increased. Almost every day terrorists were seen by someone on the estate. Rubber trees were slashed, oil palms harvested, the labour force intimidated and above all, there was the threat of an ambush at any time! All roads out of Mentakab were extremely dangerous, in fact the only safe way out was by air. In view of this, The Incorporated Society of Planters asked Malayan Airways if they could organise an air service for outlying estates. Their response was very good and a Beaver service was set up. Aircraft, carrying up to six passengers, could land on most home-made landing strips. The service was a great success.

Fishing with Archie Campbell on the Pahang River

The Gurkhas Arrive

My assistant and I now had a daily escort of four Malay Special Police from 6 a.m. until dismissal in the late afternoon. The main gates and perimeter fences at the rubber factory, oil factory, labour lines and bungalow were manned by Special Police 24 hours a day. The total Malay Special Police numbered: 3 sergeants, 9 corporals and 85 men plus two armoured cars. A platoon of British troops were also stationed on the estate from time to time. Even with this small army around us, the directors back in Edinburgh thought it wise, in view of the attack in November 1948, to employ four ex-army Gurkhas as personal bodyguards for their manager and assistant on Sungai Tekal, in addition to the Malay Police escort. The Director's wishes were duly carried out and the Gurkha bodyguards were to be with us day and night. Quarters were provided for them at the bungalow. Our daily escort now consisted of four Malay Special Police and two Gurkha bodyguards. We were all well armed with an array of weapons! News of this got around fast, according to reports taken from captured bandits. Seemingly this reduced the threat of an ambush, as it was rumoured bandit policy was to ambush only if 100% certain of success. It was also now a company directive that we should remain permanently on the estate for a period of six weeks, at the end of which we would receive six days' local leave, all expenses paid thus reducing the danger of ambush.

Our daily escort

The Sungai Tekal Film Club and The Toddy Shop

The work force at this period in time was somewhat unstable and kept changing monthly, even with the higher wages that were paid on Sungai Tekal. The changing labour force made management difficult, mainly due to the isolation of the estate and the fact that a few of the Tamils and Chinese were communist sympathisers. For that I could not blame them. I often thought, with uneasy reflections on opening a bottle of Tiger beer, the cost of that bottle was the equivalent of one man's wage for a full day's work. Unfortunately that was the way things were, change had to come.

Knowing that I would be on Sungai Tekal for the next three years, something had to be done for the work force. Apart from their religious holidays, a few sports and rare trips to the nearest town, the labour force had little in the way of recreation. In conjunction with the kanganies (foremen) and union officials, the Sungai Tekal Film Club was formed. This set-up, involving Tamil kanganies and union officials, was unique. It was frowned upon, doomed from the start by the planting community, including some Scottish Malayan planters. A committee of four Tamils was put together to run it. $2,000 was borrowed from the estate (which I was held responsible for) to buy a Bell & Howell projector (35mm) screen and loudspeakers. The labour force agreed to a deduction from their monthly wage of $1 per head. With a total labour force of over 200, the loan was paid back in a short period. A contract was taken out with the Indian Film Unit and R.K.O. Radio Studios to supply four Tamil, one Malay, one Chinese and one English film per month at a cost of $80.

The Bell & Howell projector was installed in an open-sided shed in front of the bungalow, at the lower end of the garden, within the compound of the bungalow and labour lines (workers accommodation). As the bungalow was built on the side of a bukit (hill) this part of the garden was ideal, with its gradual slope down to the perimeter security fence. The slope provided plenty of elbow room for a large audience, with a clear view of the screen which was held in place between two tall coconut palms. There was also an excellent view from the veranda of my bungalow. When John McGregor, who was acting for Mac Hunter, arrived to carry out the monthly report, a Tamil film was being shown. John being a Tamil scholar, enjoyed the show. The following month Mac Hunter resumed his monthly duties and was visiting Sungai Tekal during the screening of *Tarzan* (how apt!). He wrote in his report how amazed he was to see a film screening in the depth of the Malayan jungle. His remarks summed up precisely how isolated this location really was. In his report he gave the film club his full blessing. I enjoyed reading his reports, no matter how serious the subject they all seemed to contain a slightly boyish humour. No other estate that I knew of had a cinema (at least not for the workforce). It may not seem much in comparison with today's 'high tech' living but in 1950's Malaya this was a marvel that brought joy and excitement to all, especially to the workforce.

The Bell & Howell projector

Within a few months the club was showing a good profit. The money was spent on the children, for items such as schooling, books, radio and uniforms. On Coronation Day, 2nd June 1953, a Tamil Highland Games was held with sport of all sorts, including tossing the caber. This was followed by a goat curry, with music, dancing and free beer all round. The proceeds from the film club paid for all and similar events in the future.

The estate school children having lunch served on banana leaves

Ramasamy.
He was known as the 'engine driver' as he was responsible for
running the entire oil factory and he was extremely good at his
job

The success of the film club inspired the Tamil workers to new ideas and among other things they suggested a 'Toddy Shop' should be opened. Again this was met with disapproval by most planters. They believed it could lead to drunkenness and trouble if not properly controlled. It was put to Mac Hunter and he agreed to it, with the proviso that on the first sign of trouble it would close. There was a small duty to pay on the sale of toddy, so it was necessary to obtain a licence from Customs and Excise. Toddy is the sap from the stem of the coconut flower. The flower is initially cut off and a cup is attached to the stem to catch the sap. This is done by toddy tappers in the very early hours of the morning. The stem is tapped (a very small slice of stem cut off) every second day. The coconut area is divided into two fields to give a daily supply of sap. The last coconut palm must be tapped before 8 a.m. The tappers will then start collecting the sap at 9 a.m. and must finish by 12 noon. The sap is then taken to the Toddy Shop where it is measured and recorded for excise duty. It is then stored in Shanghai jars to be sold as toddy.

Weighing in the latex

Toddy tapping can be a dangerous occupation, as some of the palms are very high, some thirty feet plus. Daily at 2 p.m. the toddy was put on sale at a cost of 30 cents per quart and at 4.30 sharp the Toddy Shop was closed. This provided at least some solace from their hard lives, and union officials agreed with me that this was the best policy. The duty paid to Excise was 20 cents per gallon. All the toddy that had not been sold was then destroyed and thrown out – that was the law. If toddy was left to ferment over a 24-hour period its alcohol content became very high, without rigid control this could get quickly out of hand and drunkenness would prevail. In view of this the Toddy Shop was put in the hands of the Film Club Committee and apart from one incident we had no trouble.

The Toddy Shop was also making a profit, all of which went to the labour force in the form of welfare and recreation. Toddy was approved by all estate doctors as a healthy drink – I had a quart sent to the bungalow every day. By the end of the first year a permanent labour force was established and were loyal, up to a point. I didn't know it at the time, but having a stable labour force put me in good stead with the communists. This came to light some years later when several terrorists surrendered at Sungai Tekal Estate.

Killing the Wild Boar

In August and September the oil palm crop is at its peak and to cope with the extra fruit it was necessary for the oil palm factory to work overtime. Work in the factory was hard and hot, so free meals were supplied twice a day. One of the most popular meals was curried pork (wild boar). A boar had to be hunted and killed every day when the factory was on overtime. When available, iguana lizard was the overall favourite, but they were more difficult to come by. Wild boar on the other hand were to be found in large numbers on an oil palm estate and were classed as vermin. They fed on the loose fruit and any fruit bunches that were left waiting to be collected. The task of supplying the wild boar was left to Dod Cables, who cherished the assignment and became an expert hunter.

Before the Communist Emergency broke out, Tamils on the estate had regular boar hunts and kept a pack of trained hunting dogs for the purpose. The dogs were all mongrels and for their self-preservation had their ears and tails cut off, which gave them a foreboding and gruesome look, however it gave the wild boar less to bite on. When the Tamil hunters came across a herd of boar they would send in the dogs. One of the hunters would climb a tree, carrying a spear, another would stand behind the tree with a sharp axe. The dogs by this time would have selected their quarry, one large pig. The hunters would then start calling the dogs towards the tree, this would take some time. When the dogs finally got the pig under the tree the hunter would spear the pig, another hunter would split its back with the axe. Their method for dressing and cooking the pig was unique. A fire with fronds was set and the whole pig placed on it. It was then shaved of all its hair and scraped clean. While this was taking place the pig would gradually begin to inflate, no doubt due to the expanding internal gases within, until it was almost at bursting point. Then the cook, with great precision, would slit the stomach in one fast movement. With that all the inners would eject clear of the pig, leaving it as clean as a whistle. The pig was then cut up and cooked in several ways in order to suit the different palates of Tamil, Bengali and Chinese. Owing to the boar's testicle being a delicacy, a roster was kept in the office headed 'Buah Pelir' (fruit of the penis). This roster was necessary in order to stop all arguments that took place over this highly valued dish!

Burglary at Mount Pleasant

The six-day local leave was one of the only times I could really relax. It was my only time away from the relentlessly harrowing events caused by the Emergency. Leave was always something to look forward to. I made my base the Mount Pleasant Hotel in Penang. The hotel was built on a hill, with the swimming pool and main building overlooking a beautiful beach. Around the main building there were several chalets built into the hillside consisting of a sitting room on the ground floor level and a bedroom and bathroom downstairs. Che Puteh and I had a permanent booking for one every six weeks. Penang, being a small island, was more or less free of communist guerrilla activity but one still had to be vigilant. On arrival at the hotel I would hide my 455 revolver (my father's Indian Army 1915 service revolver) under the mattress.

One night, having been to a cabaret, we were late returning to the chalet and noticed the front door ajar. When we entered, I could hear noises downstairs coming from the bathroom and rushed down. The intruders had locked themselves in the bathroom which had a very small window. I retrieved my revolver from under the mattress and shouted to them to open the door. There was a lot of scuffling, so I shot off the lock and went in, but it was too late. They had managed to somehow get through the tiny bathroom window. I fired several shots at them from the window but they all managed to get away. In the next chalet to mine there just happened to be a Chief Inspector of police on honeymoon, who when he heard the gunshot came into my chalet and threatened to arrest me. Suddenly his wife came in crying – she had been robbed of her jewellery and her pistol was missing. No more was said about my arrest. Two of my shirts were missing and I found my camera on the bathroom floor.

Wild Dogs

On my way back from leave, I was to call in at our Agency House (Cumberbatch) in Kuala Lumpur and collect the four Gurkhas that had been assigned as my bodyguard. They came back with me to Sungai Tekal. The following day, their first day in service, they took part in the Wild Dog saga. That afternoon while in the estate office, working on estimates for the coming year, a kangany (foreman) from the rubber division came running into the office shouting that a pack of wild dogs were attacking goats and cattle in the grazing area. We, two Gurkhas and the kangany, got into the scout car and sped down to the grazing area. Dodd Cable had arrived first and shot four of the dogs that had killed most of the goats. It had almost been a complete massacre and the slaughtered goats lay all over the grazing area.

The dogs were now heading in the direction of the grazing near the oil palm division. By taking a short cut we arrived there before the pack. We told the herdsman to round up the goats and cattle. As we were doing this, the pack arrived on the scene and started to attack the goats. The wild dogs appeared to have no fear of man or dog and chased off the labourer's pig-hunting dogs. We shot another twelve of them before the rest of the pack dispersed. The leader of the pack was killed and the dogs scattered in all directions, the majority making for the jungle. The kangany in charge of the oil division was asked to bury the dead dogs in a deep grave. We returned to the office. These wild dogs were about 2 feet in height, their legs and underside were a light brown colour with a black back.

That evening I spoke to the police superintendent and told him about the attack. The following day Jimmy Hislop MC (Military

Cross medal), who was the Game Warden for the State of Pahang called wanting to know all about the attack and details of the dogs. He was very interested as very little was known about wild dogs in the area. He arranged for his ranger to call and pick up one of the dogs. The kangany was asked to retrieve one of the dogs from the grave. He looked bewildered and explained that he had sold the dogs to the Chinese on the estate. However we did manage to retrieve a pelt and a skull for the game ranger.

Armed, at work on the estate

More Bandit Activity

When Middleton and myself had been given the authority by the District Officer to recruit and train a Special Police Force, we were more or less a law unto ourselves. All recruits were put on the company payroll, we purchased and issued all weapons and ammunition. This was mainly shotguns as they were the only guns available at that time. In all, this was a private army of some 30 men, made up of recruits keen to have military training. However the loyalty they had shown proved, in some cases, to be false. Some defected, joining up with the Communist Guerrillas on that dark night of 8th November 1948. Although I had trusted and respected them up to this point, I had now begun to understand and sympathise with their situation. I had fought for my country during the war, but that war had ended for me in 1945, but not for the Malays. They were now simply doing as I and my pals had done, the only difference being their country was already occupied. The situation did improve when Scottish Malayan Estates hired Gurkhas (ex-service men) as personal bodyguards. Even then, I was always on the defensive and laid booby trap alarms round the bungalow bedroom. I always kept, in addition to my 38 Colt revolver, a sawn-off shotgun by my bed. I also kept a rucksack containing hard tack rations, water, two hand grenades, spare ammo and a field ambulance pack. During the day I was never without my .38 Colt revolver. These precautions lasted throughout my stay on Sungai Tekal.

Killing the Buffalo

On the last day of Bulan Puasa (Ramadan) 1953, a party of Malays from the nearby kampong of Sungai Dalam (deep river), arrived at the bungalow. We were having brunch with our visiting doctor, Dr Wilson. He had completed his monthly visit to the workforce the previous day and had spent the night with us. He would be leaving on the 3 p.m. train for Kuala Krau and Jerontut. In his spare time the doctor wrote adventure stories for a popular boys' comic. After a whisky or two, he found Sungai Tekal to be the ideal place for inspiration! During the war he had served with the Marines.

The village penghulu (chief) joined us, he needed a letter from me giving him permission to shoot one of their own buffalos. It had been causing damage to the drains on the estate, near the swamp area. Knowing that wasn't the real reason for them wanting to kill it, I jokingly said we would refer him to the District Officer for letting his buffalo stray. He laughingly replied, "Well, Tuan, there will be one less today." When asked what they were to shoot the buffalo with, they pointed to their single-barrel shotguns and produced some home-made buckshot. The penghulu added, "Perhaps Tuan can shoot it for us?" We had a large 'Savage' shotgun and some high-powered single spiral ball shot in the bungalow, used for shooting wild boar. I willingly took up the challenge. Dr Wilson wanted to see this and joined the party. A story similar to this epic appeared in a comic some weeks later, it may have been the *Rover* or something similar, I can't recall the name exactly.

Before setting off for the swamp area, the Malay alim (holy man), explained that the buffalo would be eaten at their Hari Raya (holiday) festival feast, the end of Bulan Puasa (Ramadan). First the buffalo had to be wounded, then the Alim would cut itsa throat and say special prayers. My instructions were to shoot it in the shoulder, to bring it to its knees and they would do the rest. The shooting party was growing – it now consisted of five villagers, the doctor, myself and my special police escort, along with two Gurkhas. We eventually found the buffalo herd grazing in the swamp area. The villagers selected the biggest of the bulls, shouting "Tembek itu" (shoot that one). This was not a herd of rampaging beasts, each animal was peacefully grazing and were oblivious to this great 'party of warriors'. From a safe twenty feet away, I took aim and fired. Slowly the buffalo lifted its head, gazed over as one of the villagers shouted, "Tiada kena, tiada kena" (missed it, missed it). With that blood spouted out of its shoulder and it charged off with the rest of the herd.

We all gave chase and apart from taking the doctor to Tekal Halt to catch the 3 p.m. train, the chase went on all day until dusk. Every time the buffalo stopped it was shot. One of the Gurkhas, along with a Malay guard, shot it several times with their 303 rifles. I also managed to get in another shot, but the buffalo kept on going. As darkness fell our party gave up the chase and returned to the bungalow, leaving the kampong Malays to make their final ritual killing.

The following afternoon, the same party of villagers arrived at the bungalow carrying several gifts, two of which were large chunks of buffalo meat. These were passed on to the cook. He served them for dinner that night. Seemingly, the villagers had followed the buffalo to the Sungai Pahang (the river nearby) where it lay bathing its wounds. They shot it again before cutting its throat and saying their holy prayers. As a parting gesture the penghulu presented me with the spiral ball shot which I had used to first shoot the buffalo. According to the Malays, this shot was retrieved from the shoulder bone of the buffalo, which it had shattered. That night while carving the buffalo roast, the foul smell of rotting flesh almost made me sick. The chunks of meat had been carried on a bamboo string all the way from their kampong. Meat rotted very quickly in the heat.

So much for the roast dinner. Sensibly the Gurkhas made curry with the meat they were given and said it tasted very good. Although the day had been enjoyable, I view the whole incident with mixed feelings.

Sam Sue Seller Killed in Custody

Amidst all the turbulence and disorder there is one gruesome incident I cannot forget. Mac Hunter, together with his escort, had arrived by rail jeep to carry out his monthly routine inspection, a two-day stay. It happened to be pay day and I had just finished paying out the labour force – no small task. The Malay Special Police sergeant informed me that a Chinese illicit, sam sue (rice whisky) seller was mingling with the workforce. He was on his way to arrest him.

The next morning when Hunter and I were in the office, the Malay sergeant with two Malay police and the sam sue seller arrived. Hunter told the sergeant to escort the seller to the railway halt and to wait there until Hunter arrived to escort the prisoner to Mentakab police station. When he and I arrived at the halt, I could sense an uneasy atmosphere amongst the police but there was no sign of the prisoner. To our astonishment they told us he was lying dead on the other side of the railway track. We walked over and could see that the back of his head had been blown off with buckshot. Seemingly, he had asked one of the police if he could relieve himself. On being given permission he walked across the track. One of the other policeman had not heard the request, thought he was trying to escape and shot him. Hunter and I were both shocked, to say the least! When the rail jeep arrived to pick up Hunter and his escort, the dead prisoner was strapped across the bonnet. The two Malay police who had been his escort sat in front, lying against the body. Hunter and his escort boarded the rail jeep and the party made its way to Mentakab. Twelve bodies in all, in a four-seater jeep! The rail jeep was a modified US army jeep with the road wheels replaced by rail track wheels. The next day the two Malay SP arrived back on the estate. The whole incident was recorded as death by misadventure! No red tape in those days, no human rights or compensation for the so-called 'coolies'. This was British Malaya!

Death of Malay Escort

There was another sad accident that happened to a young Malay constable. The sleeping quarters and kitchen for the sentries and escorts were built next to the servants' quarters. There were no actual beds or bunks, instead the sleeping area consisted of one long platform, the length of the building. Each sentry had his own sleeping mat and sarong. On the day of the accident, we (four Malay escorts and myself) had just returned from inspection of the rubber tapping, over an area of 100 acres, followed by a visit to the rubber factory to see the processing of the previous day's latex, a visit to the smoke house to check the temperature, through the packaging shed and back to the bungalow for brunch. The four escorts on duty retired to their quarters at the bungalow. One of the escorts was armed with a Sten gun, which can be a very dangerous weapon if the safety catch is left off, a knock or a bump can set off the firing mechanism with devastating consequences. The escort had thrown down the loaded weapon with its safety catch off, onto the sleeping platform where a comrade who had been on night duty was sleeping. The gun accidentally fired and shot his sleeping comrade. The bullet entered through his bottom and came out through his chest. Having no facilities on the estate for this sort of emergency, we immediately called the Mentakab police for the armoured plated police train to take him to hospital. The estate dresser (nurse) did what he could for him, devastatingly, the young man died on the armoured train before it reached Mentakab.

Gurkha Shoots Tapper worker

The rubber division on Sungai Tekal was called Sungai Changie (hard wood river) estate and owned by the Strathmore Rubber Company. One morning in June 1955 my round of inspection took me close to the estate boundary. A Chinese woman suddenly appeared from an overgrown plot of kampong rubber trees. Thinking she was a CT, one of the Gurkhas instinctively fired two rounds in her direction. One shot hit the bucket she was carrying. The women did not have permission to tap this overgrown plot and should not have been there.

Later, unbeknown to me, the Chinese women, who had had her bucket shot at, reported the incident to the police at Kuala Krau. She stated that a white man had shot at her. Each one of my escorts had been interrogated by the police without my knowledge. Lucky for me, they remained loyal and their Corporal Mohammed told me that the CID was trying to make a case against me for attempted murder. Apparently, the women and a Sikh CID Inspector would be visiting me, in order for the women to identify me. This left me fairly shaken.

On the day of the visit the Kuala Krau police phoned, on the pretence that a routine inspection of the police quarters was to be carried out,. They were asking for transport to meet the train at Sungai Tekal Halt. The police on the estate had no knowledge of this inspection. With this in mind, Dodd Cables and myself along with our full police escort and Gurkhas, went to meet the train. I confronted them and asked the woman to pick out the person who had shot at her. She picked out Dodd Cables! This was most convenient as Dodd was on local leave at the time of the incident. The Gurkha who did the shooting wanted to own up. I had pre-advised him to keep quiet until asked. Nothing more was said and we left them at the halt with a long wait for the 3 p.m. up train from Mentakab back to Kuala Krau.

No further action was taken regarding this incident. I was never asked about what really happened and when I spoke to Jock Neill about the case, he seemed uneasy and had nothing further to say. If it had not been for the loyalty of Mohammed and my escort the matter could have been very detrimental to me. I am greatly indebted to them.

The Monkey Man Attack

By coincidence, that same day, a distressed female worker had been taken to the estate dispensary and attended to by the dresser Mr Kau. He informed me that she had told him she had been raped by a naked 'hairy man'. On occasions male monkeys did chase women tappers. It was company policy therefore, to keep the women's tapping tasks as far away from the jungle edge as possible. From time to time there had been supposed sightings of 'hairy men', but never any proof of such a being. Some Malays believed there was a primitive race of 'hairy men' living in the limestone caves at Batu Melintang Kelantan and also that this was where the human race originated. Somewhere in the Kelantan jungle a small tribe was thought to still exist, called 'Orang Hutan' (a human being of the jungle) the same name as the orang-utan of Borneo. Perhaps, in bad light one could mistake an orang-utan for a 'hairy man'. However there are no orang-utans in Malaya; they only live wild in the jungles of Borneo and Sumatra.

When I was an assistant on Sungai Tekal Estate in early 1948, I was out hunting wild pig in part of the oil palm division which had not been reclaimed. Palm oil fruit is a favourite food of wild pig and in this neglected area was in abundance. With plenty of ground cover the area was ideal for hunting. Having just shot a pig, I was about to go and inspect my quarry, when a hairy ape-like creature appeared from behind a palm, it looked at me then bolted into the undergrowth. In those few seconds a human figure did register in my brain and memory.

Jock the 'Scottie'

When I was an assistant on Elmina Estate, Norman Alexander, the manager, gave me 'Jock' a Scottish Highland Terrier as a present. On Elmina, Jock had one of his many mishaps. A labourer's dog, a bitch, had come on heat and Jock went after her to 'chance his luck'. However, when he came back to the bungalow he was badly wounded with one of his testicles torn and hanging out. Joe Walker, a farmer's son I was staying with at the time, suggested it should be put back in its bag and stitched up. This was done, but after a few days the bag ruptured exposing the badly swollen testicle. We decided to amputate and re-stitch the bag. The operation was a success and did not effect Jock's sexual prowess in any way, although he was a sorry looking sight. There seemed to be an urgency about him, he was always on the prowl, and got into many scrapes. Before I left for home leave I had to find a home for Jock, so I gave him to the Chinese mandor (head workman) who was very fond of him. I did miss him though, we had had many exploits together.

Hens and the Musang

To get good fresh eggs on Sungai Tekal was a problem. Local eggs had a fishy smell and taste as most of them came from kampongs situated along the banks of the Sungai Pahang river and the chickens were fed fish as part of their daily feed. The only way to solve this problem was to keep a flock of healthy hens in the bungalow compound. I bought a Rhode Island Red cock from the government agriculture station, to breed with the local kampong hens. Within a short period a flock of birds of good size was established. They gave a supply of eggs and tasty chickens for the pot. The bungalow was in the oil palm division and had ample supply of palm fruit in addition to the normal chicken feed and this certainly helped to fatten the birds. Flocks of ducks, turkey and geese were also established to supply food for the table.

Supplies of food came by rail from the Singapore Cold Storage Company by mail order, but it could not be relied on since the outbreak of the Emergency. It often arrived in poor condition, due to terrorist activity. Trains could be delayed for days.

One day while out hunting wild boar I shot a jungle cock hen. I found its nest nearby with two eggs in it. These were brought back to the bungalow and put under a broody hen. When the eggs hatched, one was a cock and the other a hen. Unfortunately during a thunderstorm, the hen flew up a tree and died. The cock on the other hand grew to maturity and became leader of the flock. All the hens would follow him around. He would help the mother hens guard their chicks and scrape for food for them, unlike the Rhode Island Red who would chase the chicks away if they came near his food. Every time the Rhode Island Red crowed, the small jungle cock would fly at him and chase him around the yard. Unfortunately the oncoming chickens, although very healthy, were much smaller. This jungle cock would, on occasions, fly off and be away for days at a time. On his return the hens would become very excited and go off the lay!

I was once given a gift from a Chinese contractor, Too Ha Toon, a hen with feathers protruding out the wrong way, concealing most of its head. Much to our amusement this made it look like we had a headless chicken running about. Mac Hunter came to visit, he named it Ayan Gila (mad chicken) and suggested we should curry it. Having poultry did attract many predators such as snakes and iguana lizards, but the most menacing was the musang (large civet) that sought its prey by night. If it got into the hen house it would kill many birds but only take one. They are very vicious creatures and had been known to kill watchdogs. Musang have a pungent smell and the chickens could sense their approach long before they got near the henhouse. The noise of the hens would alert all at the bungalow of their approach. Two betel nut palms were growing in the hen-run, and when musang were disturbed during a raid they would scamper up one of the slim palms and take cover in the fronds. To get rid of this menace, I rigged a 22 rifle up with a torchlight. This illuminated the eyes of the musang, and gave me a sure target to shoot at. I shot several of them this way. One night I heard scuffling under the bungalow (the bungalow was built on stilts), the noise alerted the bungalow guards who found that 'Jock' had killed a musang. He had been used to worrying dead musangs which had been shot and this may have given him confidence, but to kill one was a remarkable feat as most dogs ran in fear from them.

The Eagle

Another predator was the Lang (eagle). One, the Geruda (eagle of the gods) gave the most trouble. Landing on a palm near the bungalow, it would watch and wait. As soon as a hen strayed from the flock, it would strike with one swift swoop and the hen would be gone. Watching this, I decided to try falconry and asked one of the Orang Sakai (aborigine) if he could find a young eagle or an egg. Some days later the Sakai brought in an egg of the Garuda, which was put under a broody hen. In ten days the chick broke through the shell, so I put it in a box containing rough wool and left it in the transmitter room below the bungalow. The young eagle was fed on chicken liver. It grew quickly but lacked strength. Before it was fully grown it disappeared, probably taken by a snake. This ended the falconry.

Chan Lee and the Tiger

While on the subject of eggs there is another story to tell. Chan Lee was an Chinaman of the old school, hard working, polite, with a good sense of humour. He was very thin. Chan had worked on Sungai from the early days and took part in the raft episode of 1927 with McIntosh. On his retirement, he was given a room in the bungalow's servant quarters and put on the bungalow payroll. Chan did the odd jobs around the bungalow. Every Sunday he would walk to Kuala Krau to attend the Sunday market where he would buy the weekly supply of vegetables and eggs before we had the hens. It was Chan's highlight of the week, as he would meet up with some of his old cronies. The round trip was approximately nine miles and part of the way was by a jungle footpath. Chan made a full day of his visit to Kuala Krau, leaving the bungalow at daybreak and returning just before dusk. He told me that on one of his return journeys he heard the loud purring of a tiger. He stood stock still. The tiger sniffed round him, gave him a slight push and wandered off. Before Chan had finished telling his story, he smiled saying that this was not all together true – "Being scared, I farted, the tiger pushed me and wandered off." I exploded with laughter. Chan's punch line was, "Was it the smell that did it or am I too thin?" He walked away, shaking his head and laughing.

Many more tigers were roaming the countryside, than we ever saw. At that time we were hearing less about them than ever. 'Belong' (Malay for stripes/tiger) were finding all the deer, wild pig and Seladang (large jungle ox) and other game that they needed for survival, without leaving their natural habitat. Consequently they did not have the incentive to venture into kampongs in search of domestic cattle and humans. Before the Emergency, when a gun licence was easy to obtain, hunting by man was common and deprived the tigers of their usual prey.

Chan had been on the estate for years and told me how the flat area of Sungai Pahang valley was flooded to a depth of 30 feet in 1927. Seemingly Sungai Tekal was completely flooded. The story goes that the manager at the time, Hamish McIntosh, dismantled his wooden bungalow, along with the labour huts, in order to build rafts. He floated the complete labour force and their families downstream to Temerloh and safety. The rafts were linked together, train fashion. McIntosh sat in a large rattan chair on the leading raft, with a 12 bore shotgun on his knee, shooting at any snakes and crocodiles that ventured anywhere near the rafts. Below the rattan chair was a case of whisky. One of the survivors of this event was Chan Lee.

Teck Seng

The last job Chan did for me before going home on long leave was to bag up empty beer bottles. The empties from over a three-year period. The beer had been ordered from Teck Seng a Mentakab Merchant and a dear friend. There was a deposit charge of 3 cents on each bottle, Chan bagged the bottles at a rate of 25 bottles per gunny sack. The bottles had been stacked around the servants' quarters, missing the windows and doors and up round the back section of the bungalow. Teck sent a cheque for $277 being the pay for 9,233 bottles in 369 gunny sacks. Two railway wagons were required for this task. 8–9 bottles (Tiger Beer) were drank on Sungai Tekal a day. Considering the friends, business associates and police officers that would visit Sangei Tekal, the amount of beer drunk was

5th May

Dear John,

Very many thanks
Carolyn and I both enjoyed
no small measure how very
and their hives here for ye

with my best wishes

e, London N1 2AN

0 7226 8866

2017.

for lending this book.
ding it. It brings home in
urageous the Malayan Planters
s on end. Remarkable really.

Jonas Lewis

reasonable. To cover this additional household expenditure the company paid a substantial entertainment allowance.

Snakes, Rats and Knotted Tailed Cats

It was a belief among the Tamil oil palm harvesters that every palm had a family of rats living in the upper fronds. As the oil palm fruit ripen all year round, the rats had a constant supply of food on the doorstep, so to speak.

The rats were smaller than their European cousins and had a large pouch under the tail which contained fat. Every six months, six rats were caught and sent alive to the Agricultural Research Dept. in Kuala Lumpur to be tested for typhoid among other things.

With every palm having this family of rats it meant easy pickings for the common cobra. With the threat of a cobra lurking in the palm the harvester had to be on his guard at all times. The harvesting was done with an axe, a broad-faced light axe rather like a smaller version of an old executioner's axe.

One or two fronds were cut off to get at the fruit bunch before it could be harvested. Some of the old palms were up to 25 feet high. The ladder used was a single bamboo stem with rungs through it at every foot. Occasionally a cobra would strike and spit venom into the face of the harvester, which would render him blind for a few days. This was one of the many occupational hazards the harvester had to endure.

There was one incident when a King Cobra was seen slithering around the oil palm factory and I was called on to shoot it, however when I got there it had disappeared. Later that day it was seen again, coiled around one of the statues in the Hindu Temple. When I went to shoot it, I was told by one of the labour force that there was no need to do so, as it was repenting for the trouble it had caused and would not return to the factory again. I took heed of this, and in fact it was never seen again.

Another common snake to be found was the python. By far the largest snake in Malaya, it could grow up to 20 feet long. One of the women tappers came across a snake of this size. She had just finished tapping 200 trees and before collecting the latex, had sat down to rest on a hardwood jungle timber. These timbers did not burn or rot away when the jungle was first cleared, but were mainly used for bridges. To the tapper's surprise, she noticed a large python lying asleep next to the timber. She calmly finished collecting the latex and at the weigh-in reported the snake to the kerani (clerk) in charge. By the time I got to hear about it, most of the labour force had the news. When I arrived a gang of Tamil women, who had been cutting undergrowth in a neighbouring field, had hacked the snake to pieces. A fully grown wild pig was found inside the snake. Both snake and pig made an excellent meal, that evening, for the rubber section of workers.

As the bungalow was in the oil palm division it was also infested with rats. The cook could not put any food on the table before we sat down to a meal. If he did, the rats would be there first. One night I got out of bed to get a drink and I ate a bit of ham from the fridge. Later I was awakened by small tongues licking my thumb and fingers, something was scampering over my chest, it was rats. I jumped up and shook them off. Then went back to bed and sleep, only to be awakened again by the same thing. This time I threw one of them against the bedroom wall as it bit into my nail. I ran to the bathroom and washed my hand with disinfectant. The swelling went down in a few days and all was well.

To set traps for the rats was of little use, as there were so many of them. The bungalow cat did keep some of them at bay. He was a tom Malay cat with a handsome face, but like most cats in Malaya he had an ugly knot at the end of his tail that looked like he had a deformity of some kind. It was off-putting to stroke him. No one seemed to know why the knot should be there, it looked more like a hazard than an asset.

An Elephant at the Door

Now and again a herd of elephants would pass through the plantation and there was always damage to put right, but usually nothing serious. On one occasion a large stray elephant caused considerable damage in the bungalow compound. Che Puteh and I were awakened, that night, by the Malay sentries shouting "Gajah, Gajah" (elephant) and to our astonishment the bungalow was shaking. When I looked out of the bedroom window, sure enough there was a large elephant scratching itself against the bungalow, I could almost touch it. What could we do? A wild elephant is a formidable beast. We went out the back and spoke to the sentries and decided to stay quiet with the hope that it would move on. However, Jock my Scottie was running about barking, this upset the elephant and it charged at Jock with its trunk held high. The elephant had burst through the bulldog mesh fence at the foot of the bungalow compound. It had been raining heavily that evening and the ground was soft, making the fence easy for the elephant to push through. The beast was now roaming round the compound trying to find a way out, having tried to push the fence over in several places. We took cover in the kubus (pillboxes).

During the rampage, the chicken house was knocked about and hens, geese, duck and turkeys were everywhere. The elephant finally made a successful charge and broke through the bulldog fence, out into the plantation and away. Speaking to the sentries the next morning, they had known something was wrong when the perimeter security lights failed. Mat bin Yousaff, the Guard Commander, summed up the situation saying, "This will be a tale to tell the grandchildren." During that night, for a moment or two, it was indeed frightening. A mad elephant charging round the compound was no joke! A few days later I spoke to the Game Ranger at Kuala Lumpar about the incident. He said there had been a report of a rogue elephant in our area causing damage to some of the kampongs. Seemingly, this elephant had one of its tusks growing into its head and because of this was going mad. We had not had time to see if the tusk on our elephant was deformed. We were only too glad when it broke free of the compound!

A casualty of this skirmish was a pet bear cub which had escaped from its hutch after it had been knocked over. The gardener found the bear the next morning clinging to a small palm. The cub was extremely upset but calmed down within the next few days. It had previously been rescued from death when its mother had been caught by the leg in a pig-trap and speared to death by Tamil hunters. We arrived on this cruel scene just in time to save the cub. Pig-traps of this type were like large rabbit traps, but they were lethal and could cut a man's leg off, so they were banned by law. The two Tamils who set the trap had to be dismissed and taken to Mentakab Police Station to be charged. From the start the baby bear had been fed on warm condensed milk, followed by bread mixed with condensed milk and fruit. It grew fast and seemed to be healthy and friendly to all the bungalow staff. It was a young female. When it grew older every time a women approached the bungalow it would growl and get upset. Maybe it was jealousy. As it grew it became dangerous and strong, so strong that it could puncture a milk can with its claw and suck it dry in seconds. The time had come to find another home for the bear. The area Game Warden,

Jimmy Hislop MC, was informed and a game manager took the bear to an animal sanctuary where it could mix with other bears before being released into the jungle.

Poisoned Elephants

Man's destruction of nature for profit was cruel and endless. Looking back I recall a sad event regarding two elephants. 'Lallang', a vigorous growing grass of the couch variety, but much stronger, grew to a height of three feet. It was a widespread and very troublesome weed. To dig out this deep-rooted weed was costly and every piece of the root had to be removed. ICI Chemists came up with the answer, spraying the Lallang with 2½ % solution of sodium arsenic ten times at three-day intervals. Very successful in killing the Lallang but not so good for the wild life, not to mention the labourers who did the actual spraying, many of whom came out in sores and had trouble breathing. Protective clothing of a sort was provided but was of little use. The putrid smell of dying grass was foul. After the first few sprays there was an uncanny sweet smell which unfortunately attracted wildlife. We were told by ICI soil chemists that this was due to the salts in the sodium arsenic. More deadly than this was 'Teppol' which ICI had developed. This made the mixing water wetter, so more sodium arsenic stuck to the blades of grass.

One night a herd of elephants passed through a sprayed area leaving their tracks everywhere. Two days later, a drainage contractor came across two dead elephants in the swamp. One of them was like a barrage balloon with its stomach full of gas. It was believed that they must have eaten the deadly sprayed grass which made them thirsty. They went to the swamp to drink and drank themselves to death. A grave was dug for them. I never did like spraying with sodium arsenic and did as little as possible. It was certainly not suited for a place like Sungai Tekal deep in the jungle of Pahang.

Struck by Lightning

Electrical storms were common and usually occurred in the late afternoon, before rain or just after. A daily security procedure was to make a radio call to Mentakab police station at 5 p.m. which was entered in the Radio Log Book and checked by the Duty Sergeant. My bungalow was built on stilts 8 feet high; the transmitter was kept below in a specially constructed room, giving easy access to the bungalow police guards. Apart from the routine call, the radio was only used in emergencies. As the telephone wires were often cut, emergencies were a common occurrence.

One afternoon during an electrical storm, I switched off the transmitter and was walking away; suddenly, I received a terrific blow to my back which knocked me off my feet, my shoes were so hot they were almost on fire. The bungalow gardener on his nightly job of rounding up the poultry saw the flash. It lit me up like an electric lamp. All down my left side was black and blue for days.

One night sometime before this event a special police guard was killed by a lightning bolt. Within the bungalow stockade there were four kubus (a type of pillbox) placed at strategic points in case of an attack by the CT. The sentry was stationed at the main kubu after making his rounds of the bungalow compound. In the kubu, was a field telephone linked to the oil palm factory, which was the headquarters of the Sungai Tekal police force. That night there had been heavy rain and the police sentry, having made his rounds, had gone back to the kubu and sat next to the telephone still wearing his wet cape. The reason for his death, we believe, was that his wet cape was touching the telephone receiver when the lightning struck the wires, burning out both receivers and killing the sentry outright. The other Malay constable on duty at headquarters, although badly shaken by the exploding receiver was not hurt.

With regards to my lightning episode, I was told by an electrical engineer that the lightning had probably struck the transmitter aerial and that the earth wire from the transmitter was not large enough to take all the lightning charge to earth and the balance of the charge struck me. After these two incidents, we made sure all earth connections on the transmitter and all telephones were of ample capacity. The odd thing was that there was no damage to the transmitter. Did the bolt that hit me save the transmitter?

Woo Ka Sim and Comrade Surrender

With the coming of the new year 1954, the Mentakab district was by far the worst area in Malaya for Chinese terrorist activity. Hardly a day passed without some incident, ambush, slashing of rubber trees, and now, illicit harvesting of oil palm fruit bunches. Using the most primitive method of oil extraction one bunch of fruit would yield approx 2½ lbs of oil. On one raid alone some 200 bunches were stolen. Palm is an edible oil and can be used in the preparation of food.

The jungle headquarters and hospital for the 2nd Battalion of the Malayan People's Anti-British Army was now somewhere in the Mentakab area. Two Chinese terrorist members of the notorious 32nd Independent Platoon, Woo Ka Sim and his comrade surrendered to me in June 1954. They had been in charge of some sakais (Aborigines) who were helping with the illicit harvesting of palm oil fruit. A reward of $2800 was paid out by Jock Neill, Chief of Police in Mentakab, for the capture of the two terrorists. This 'blood money' was paid into the film club account for the welfare of the labour force.

Woo Ka Sim and comrade surrender

The Day After Pay Day

The only official holiday for the Tamil labour force on the plantations, apart from Diwali festival was the day after pay day. The second day of each month. It was a hard life for the Tamil labourers, not far off slavery. I don't know if things changed quickly for the Tamils after Malayan Independence, I have my doubts. This was the way plantations were run in British Malaya. However, this was not the Malay way of life and very few Malays worked on plantations. The main labour being Tamils and a few Chinese sub-contractors. The Tamil workers came from the Malabar coast of India to work on the Malayan plantations. On their one day off, the whole labour force would dress up and make their way to the nearest town or village. This would happen throughout Malaya. However having no roads to Sungai Tekal, the whole labour force would gather at Sungai Tekal Halt to catch the 9 a.m. down train to Mentakab. It was a half-hour journey under normal conditions. The return train was at 2 p.m., this giving them a four-hour stop in Mentakab for shopping etc. It was said you could always hear a Tamil before you saw him! This was certainly the case when the train arrived back at Sungai Tekal Halt. Most Tamil men liked a drink or two, and there was plenty of cheap sam sue (rice whisky) in town. As the crow flies, our bungalow was half a mile from the halt and when the train arrived we could hear them disembark, it was like the 'Hampden Park roar'.

Diwali Holiday

The Tamil labour force only had one day official annual holiday. This was Diwali, a major Hindu festival honouring Lukshmi the goddess of wealth and takes place in the autumn. Tamils give each other presents, there is feasting, the lighting of lamps and dancing. Like their European counterparts, unfortunately, some Tamil men got drunk and sick. Diwali was given a bad name by the British colonials. They named it, in Tamil 'Allour Perinall' (this may not be the correct spelling as my knowledge of the Tamil language has diminished over the years), Holiday of the Drains. Choice words coming from us – the British – as we, on the whole drank ten times more alcohol than any poor Tamil labourer ever did. It brought to mind a Robert Burns' quote that was well used in my own family, especially by my mother:

> "O wad some pow'r the giftie gie us
>   To see oursels as others see us!
> It wad frae monie a blunder free us,
>   An foolish notion.
>   *Robert Burns*

97

My own children are well coached in this saying!

Now that the film club was successful and carrying a large credit surplus, the committee wanted some of the cash to finance most of the Diwali celebrations. We all agreed. This would prevent the labourers getting into debt, which had happened every previous year causing many problems.

The Hindu temple on the estate was given an overdue facelift. A number of goats were purchased for the curry, several crates of beer and all sorts of provision necessary for a good feast. All toddy drunk between 2 p.m. and 4 p.m. was free. A troupe of Tamil musicians and entertainers was booked for the day. The festivities were started at dawn, first by the giving of gifts, followed by chanting at the temple, which went on most of the day. By mid-afternoon several women had gone into a complete trance and were dancing around and pushing needles, the size of knitting needles through their stomachs, cheeks and ears. Two kanganies also took part in this strange ritual. Pushing skewers through their hands, they also seemed to be in the same sort of trance, but more serious in their approach. I must say there was no sign of injury and no blood anywhere. The feasting and dancing went on well into the night, but the next morning all was back to normal. The women who had skewered themselves were back with their gangs as if nothing had happened the previous day.

CHAPTER 12

Surrendering Bandits

During this period the communists had good supply lines up to Siam and beyond. They also had so-called 'rest camps' in Siam, for the Malayan communist troops. This was hard to believe, but true. The Siam government, at the time, turned a blind eye to this. In addition, there was said to be a communist training camp on the border, with 300 Chinese recruits at any one time.

A patrol from the Hampshire Regiment were passing through Sungai Tekal in pursuit of CTs. We gave them a chicken diner, a beer and they slept that night below the bungalow. Some time later I received a letter of thanks from their CO with an invitation to their Mess in Winchester, should I ever be in Winchester.

Hampshire Regiment

North Rhodesian Regiment

In view of the CT activity in and around the estate, the district war committee, in Temerloh, decided to station a full company of the 1st North Rhodesian Regiment on the estate. The site chosen was alongside the dam, close to the rubber factory. The company commander was Captain John Hickman, a white Rhodesian; subordinate to him was a lieutenant, two 2nd lieutenants and an RSM also all white, the rest of the company were all black Rhodesians fresh out from Rhodesia. (Hickman would eventually become Chief of Staff in the UDI Rhodesian Army.) Before any patrols took place, most of the black Rhodesians went down sick with sunburn. I could not believe this, until I met the battalion medical officer who visited the camp to examine the sick men and who confirmed that indeed, they were suffering due to the sudden change in climate. Rhodesia is dry and hot in contrast to Malaya being damp, humid and very warm. Within a fortnight all was well. Regular patrols and sorties were sent out to track down and engage the communists. Finding the terrorist was a difficult and soul-destroying task. Often it was the hunter being hunted and led into an ambush. In some areas the jungle was so dense a man would be invisible at fifteen feet. The enemy couldn't be seen until you almost stepped on them. Often a patrol's daily progress was measured in yards, instead of miles. Heavy rain, jungle foot rot, and the feeling that an unseen terrorist may have you in his gun sights, made the whole operation nerve-racking. By hitting, running and vanishing, some 5,000 communist guerrillas tied up 140,000 soldiers and police. That was jungle warfare.

The Pahang jungle is the most inhospitable place imaginable – leeches, mosquitoes, scorpions and snakes are commonplace. It is damp and sultry and where the sun is blocked out by giant trees and creepers, a forbidding zone. All these conditions alone are hard enough to fight, without looking for CTs. They were well-trained jungle troops and had many techniques for coping with the jungle and using it to their advantage.

British patrols used Aborigine trackers from Sarawak and Borneo to help hunt down the CTs. The British government had stopped the practice of cutting the hands and heads off dead terrorists for identification when bringing them out of the jungle. The trackers were still permitted to take the scalps of the dead terrorists.

At Elmina Estate, on one occasion, a patrol brought out a dead CT. I pointed out to the lieutenant that I thought the dead man looked rather old to be a CT as he was bald. The lieutenant explained that the dead man had been scalped by the Dayak, who had the scalp hanging from his belt. I was shocked but not surprised. Iban and Dayaks were known to be 'head hunters'. This old custom was still being practised in Borneo and Sarawak at the time.

Alexander Gray Killed, 1955

June was not a good month for Pahang as more police and civilians were killed than terrorists. Sad to say, a neighbour of mine and fellow Scot, Cyril Alexander Gray, was ambushed and killed by the Communist 32nd Independent Platoon, commanded by the notorious Ah Chuan, known as the Director of Operation in the area. This independent platoon operated in the Bentong, Mentakab, Kerdau and Kuala Krau areas. Unfortunately for us, they were equipped with an array of weapons most suitable for jungle warfare. Ah Chuan seemed to be informed and always had a well-calculated plan when laying an ambush or making a raid.

The lurking danger of communist subversion was always a problem, coming clearly to the surface in June and July when several estates in the area suffered a series of disastrous strikes, augmented by communist-led organisations. The wages on Sungai Tekal were higher than other estates, partly due to its remote location. Union officials achieved little success with the labour force and fortunately no strikes took place on Sungai Tekal.

Wong Meng Surrenders

Since the Emergency was declared in June 1948, Sungai Tekal had endured a virtually permanent state of siege. CT aggression took the form of ambushes, intimidation of workers, attacks on bungalows and factories, slashing of rubber trees, illicit harvesting, sabotage, desertion, fire and murder. Arrival of the Rhodesian troops did little to ease CT activity in the area. Nevertheless, success did come their way, but not without loses.

Events began on 2nd May 1955 in the jungle headquarters of the 32nd Independent Platoon of the Malayan People's Anti-British Army, at Kerdau, some four miles south of Sungai Tekal Estate. The CT, Koon Kaw had been found guilty of 'wavering' by a communist jury, at a jungle trial. He was executed by stabbing. It was carried out by Ah Chong, Assistant Platoon Commander, known as the 'Executioner'. Ah Chong had a long list of murders to his name. Four days after this, a comrade named Wong Meng, disgusted with communist injustice, surrendered at Kerdau Police Station. Information he provided helped in launching an operation to route the CT from their camp near Kerdau. This task was allocated to the Rhodesian troops stationed at Sungai Tekal. On 12th May, a battle took place between the Rhodesians and the CT (32nd Independent Platoon), in the jungle, near Kerdau. The Rhodesians charged forty CT in their camp, killing five and wounding eight. A British Officer, Lieutenant K.A. Hensley who was commanding the patrol, was killed. Seemingly, he was shot in the back whilst standing up to get a better firing position. Sergeant Mountain, a black Rhodesian, took over command of the patrol. The CT killed were identified as Siew Cheng, Ah Kuan, Lee Kaw, Al Liva and Boon Wah who was the paymaster for the Pahang branch of the MP Anti-British Army. It was rumoured he carried $10,000 on his person. The battle split the CT, some moved towards the town of Raub.

Ah Sek and Comrade Surrender

Friday 27th May was my assistant Dodd Cable's birthday. Captain John Hickman, the RSM and a 2nd Lieutenant had been invited to the bungalow for drinks and dinner to celebrate. The party went on till late and all the guests stayed for breakfast. At about 5 a.m. I went out back to the servants' quarters to wake the cook. Imagine my surprise when two CT walked through the back gate, into the full beam of the security floodlight. They raised their hands above their heads, shouting, "Sahaya serahkan dire" (I surrender). The CTs, fearing the Ghurkhas, and knowing they were stationed at the bungalow did not want to surrender until a European was present. They had been waiting all night for me to appear. One of the CT, Sam Ah Sek, said they had been apprehensive about the strange music they heard coming from the bungalow. Dodd was from Aberdeen and had a large collection of Scottish country music including some pipe bands, which he had been playing at full volume, all night, to celebrate his birthday!

The guard commander, a Malay police sergeant, was called and the CT interrogated. At this stage, John Hickman and the RSM left for their base camp at the rubber factory, leaving the 2nd Lieutenant asleep in the chair. Sam Ah Sek said he and his comrade had been assigned to escort Ah Chong (the 'Executioner') to a communist jungle hospital. Ah Chong had been wounded in the chest during the battle on 12th May. On arrival, they found the hospital had been burnt down by a Rhodesian fighting patrol. He said they then made their way to Sungai Tekal in search of food. At the jungle edge of the plantation, Sam Ah Sek and his comrade turned on the wounded Ah Chong, slashing his head, neck and arm with a parong and left him there to die. They then concealed their weapons, and made their way to the bungalow to surrender. Dodd and I, with our regular Malay police escort, plus the Gurkhas and the Malay police sergeant, set off with the two CTs to find Ah Chong and recover the hidden weapons. We found the weapons but the only trace of Ah Chong, was a trail of blood leading back into the jungle!

During our absence, Jock Neill, Chief of Police, Mentakab area, with the Commanding Officer of the North Rhodesian Regiment, had arrived at the bungalow and were waiting for our return. As we walked up the hill toward the bungalow, I heard the CO exclaim to Jock Neill, "Who-the-hell-is-this?" Dodd and I were wearing sarongs, the Gurkhas in black uniform, the Malays were in green, all of us armed to the teeth. We must have looked a lawless bunch.

Jock Neill made the formal introduction. The CO was not in a good mood having found one of his young 2nd Lieutenants asleep in a chair. He became most belligerent, blaming me for the lieutenant's. condition. I asked him to leave! Jock stepped in calming what could have been an unpleasant situation. We calmed down, then arranged for the armoured train. After refreshments, the party left for Mentakab along with the two CT prisoners.

During the period of duty when a company of the North Rhodesian were billeted on Sungai Tekal the Colonel-in-Chief of Malaya, General Bourne and his staff visited Sungai Tekal. They arrived by helicopter, landing on the bukit (hill) where the manager's bungalow once stood. Captain Hickman and I were there to meet them. The estate supplied the transport, an armoured Land Rover and a Morris scout car to take them to the Rhodesian encampment at the rubber factory.

Ah Chong

The following day, Sunday 29th May, on the way down to the office, to our astonishment, sitting at the roadside, head in hands was Ah Chong. He was some 100 yards from the main gate of the oil palm factory compound and so badly wounded, barely alive and could not move. We lifted him into the armoured Land Rover and returned to the bungalow. He was in a terrible state. We offered him food but he only wanted a drink of milk. His shirt and trousers were stiff from dried blood, he had a rag round his head and neck, he was moving with lice and maggots, but only complained about the large parong wound to his upper arm. The estate dresser gave him first aid and removed the rag from his head, revealing a hole the size of a tea cup. Part of his scalp was hanging over his left ear. The blow from the parong had cut through hair, skin and bone. His throbbing brain was alarming to see. We shaved his head to get rid of the lice and maggots; although the razor nicked his head in several places, there was no blood to be seen. His scalp was left hanging over his ear and a bandage was put round his complete head. We thought replacing that part of his skull would have caused further damage.

Mr Kau the dresser (doctor/nurse) in his dispensary on the estate

The dresser cut the blood-stiff shirt off his back revealing gunshot wounds, which we plugged with cotton wool. As we removed his shirt, part of his right breast fell out, we put this back and dressed the wound as best we could. We made him as comfortable as possible. In the afternoon the Mentakab police arrived and Ah Chong was taken to hospital under police guard. I didn't think he would survive. He refused to sign the surrender document which would have pardoned him, sticking to his beliefs and remaining a communist. The endurance of some of the Chinese will always amaze me, but I didn't have much hope for Ah Chong surviving such extensive injuries.

The following week Jock Neill returned to the estate to pay out the reward of $4,600 in respect of the three CTs. This was the second time that Jock Neill had paid out a reward to me. The first time was for Woo Ka Sim and his comrade. Money from the rewards was put into the estate film club account and used for welfare, mainly for the children and the estate school.

Some weeks later at one of the planters' security meetings, held by Jock Neill in Mentakab, I learned that Ah Chong had survived. I suggested paying him a visit in hospital, with a view to persuading him to denounce communism. We hoped for him to sign the surrender document in exchange for a full pardon. I was issued with a hospital police pass and took some fruit, drinks and food. He had a private room, guarded by two police constables day and night. On entering the ward, I was amazed to see Ah Chong sitting up right on the bed with his legs crossed. When he saw me, he jumped off the bed and with a broad smile greeted me in Malay "Tabek Tuan," (Greetings Sir). What a recovery! He thanked me for the help we had given him. When I got round to asking him why he would not sign the surrender document in exchange for amnesty, his answer was short and to the point. "I am a true communist and will never denounce it and I will stand by my flag." He ended our meeting with, "Terima kaseh" (Thank you), "Salamat jalan Tuan" (Safe journey Sir). On my return from home leave in Jan 1956, I was told that Ah Chong had been tried, found guilty and hanged in September 1955. That same year Malaya held its first 'democratic election'. Representation by Malaya's Communist Party was refused by the authorities.

Sergeant Mountain and the Missing $10,000

Since the battle of 12th May, Sergeant Mountain and his platoon had been drinking heavily. On several occasions, it was reported, they had entered the labour lines and pestered some of the women. The Malay Special Police sergeant had also reported that a Malay wife of a constable had been accosted by several drunk Rhodesians. This was a serious misdemeanour. It was extremely disrespectful to insult a Malay woman or mock the Malay religion. This of course applies to all cultures, but it was not overlooked by Malay people, at least not in those days. Prior to this, at Kerdau, a Chinese storekeeper and his whole family were slaughtered by a Malay man who ran amok. The storekeeper was believed to have insulted the Malay man's wife, over a shopping debt. Acts like this were not uncommon and it was not considered a crime in Malayan law, rather an affair of the heart. The word 'amok' (in murderous frenzy) is a Malay word. Coincidentally, at Kerdau railway station, I witnessed the loading of the slaughtered Chinese family. The Malay man who slaughtered them was also on the platform. He was handcuffed and, had a dog-like collar round his neck attached to a long pole, held by two Malay police. The dead Chinese family were in wicker baskets, which were mainly used for the transporting of live pigs. It was all a very gruesome sight. With 45 well-armed Malay police on the plantation, the situation was volatile. To remedy this, all the Rhodesians were confined to camp at the rubber factory.

With this problem more or less resolved, John Hickman invited Dodd and I to the small Officers' Mess at the rubber factory camp for a regimental dinner. Whilst we were dining we were told that a disturbance had just broken out amongst the workers in the oil palm division, involving some Rhodesian troops. John called for the RSM who, in addition to his side weapon, armed himself with a pick axe handle. We then went to investigate and found Sergeant Mountain smashing a piano accordion against a palm. Several members of his platoon were fighting drunk. Hanging from Sergeant Mountain's waist was a bag which was confiscated. The bag was packed with large dollar bills – we were told he had taken it from the communist pay master Boon Wah who had been killed in the battle of 12th May. Sergeant Mountain had taken over command of the patrol following the death of Lieutenant Hensley. This solved the mystery of the missing $10,000 and the drunken binges of Sergeant Mountain's platoon!

Captain John Hickman became a Major General in the Rhodesian Army. When Ian Smith broke off all ties with the UK and declared UDI in November 1965 I was told that John was made Chief of Staff of the UDI Army.

Jock Neill

When Jock Neill was paying out rewards or when I was passing on information regarding CT activity he often said jokingly, "I think you must be in cahoots with the communists." The labour force on Sungai Tekal was also stable, which was unusual in that part of Pahang, this too seemed to perplex him. In later years, I have come to believe that his comments were a true supposition of what he was really thinking. I surmise, this could have been instigated by the fact that a senior Chief Inspector, on loan from Hong Kong Police and his Malay assistant, were sent to make a report on the, so-called, suspicious communist activity around the estate. They were to interrogate Sergeant Mountain's platoon about the killing of Boon Wah, Pay Master of the Pahang branch of the MPABA, and the cash stolen from him.

The Chief Inspector told me, in strict confidence, part of his brief was to make a confidential report on my assistant and myself as we were under suspicion. However, this was unfounded and the subsequent reports were all fine. He also brought up the subject of the lost medal recommendations from November 1948. Seemingly they had been approved, but added, there would be little chance of me receiving a police medal as my police report, which he had received from Jock Neill, stated that I had been fined £5 at Forfar Sheriff Court in 1943 for missing Home Guard Parades (Dad's Army). I am told a clean sheet is needed before a police medal can be awarded.

Jock Neil was always in uniform, shorts and shirt with knee-high socks and swagger stick. The first thing that struck you when you walked into Jock's office was how tidy it was. He sat at a large desk, with only a telephone and a framed copy of a letter written by the Duke of Wellington to the Minister of War just before the Battle of Waterloo. It stated that if he, the Duke, 'sat down to answer all the unnecessary correspondence he received, there would be no time left to fight the war.' Having read it, I laughed. Jock pointed to the dustbin close by and said, "That's my filling cabinet." I believe that the Hong Kong CID Chief's report regarding Tan's and my efforts and the recommendations for our medals, ended up in this 'filling cabinet'! With hindsight, I don't think Jock was keen on planters, he must have seen us an unruly bunch with too much of a free rein. Some of us were 'too in with the natives' for his liking!

If I remember correctly, Jock was from the Isle of Skye and joined the army at the age of fourteen as a Drummer Boy. When discharged in 1946, he held the rank of Lieutenant Colonel. He then joined the Palestine police and in September 1948 came to Malaya as a Police Sergeant and quickly promoted to Chief Inspector. Jock was single and when he first took over at Mentakab and Temerloh districts he stayed in the Temerlah Rest House, a government-run hostel. As there were no hotels in outlying areas the government built hostels throughout Malaya, mainly for European travellers. The accommodation and food was good and a reasonable price. They were also used as meeting places for planters.

On one occasion I stayed in the Temerlah Rest House and one of the other guests was Dr Wilson, our visiting Medical Officer. We were sitting having a beer when Jock Neill walked in and joined us, he put his brief case down by his chair. Jock fancied himself as an 'oil painter' and the walls of the Rest House were decorated with some of his work. He got up to adjust one of the paintings, stood back and looked at it and asked us what we thought of the it. The usual remarks were made and shortly after Jock left the room.

When he returned he said, as he switched off a tape recorder in his brief case (the first tape recorder I had seen), "Now I will really know what you both think of my paintings." As the tape started to play, the doctor picked it up and threw it out of the open window. It smashed to pieces on the concrete driveway. He looked Jock straight in the eye and said, "Don't you ever do a sly thing like that in my company." Jock left the room. He never appeared for breakfast the next day. Mind you, the doctor had said amongst other things, that he had seen better art in a kindergarten!

CHAPTER 13
Puck, Spells and Menachie

Meeting Puck

Looking east over the valley of the Sungai (river) Pahang from the bukit (hill) on which the manager's bungalow once stood (before it was abandoned and dismantled due to the Emergency) are two limestone hills which rise straight out of the jungle, known locally as Bukit Hantu (ghost hills). The hills consist of large caves. In fact the hills are hollow and are home to multitudes of Keluang (fruit bats). In the morning when shrouded in mist, the hills look like some medieval castle guarding the Sungai Pahang valley.

The caves in Bukit Hantu contained tons of bat guano which had mounted up over thousands of years and was there for the taking. A survey was required into the possibility of mining the bat guano. Before any inspection could be carried out, permission had to be obtained from the district officer and the police. Once permission was given, a contract was made with the Home Guard Commander, a Mr Hugh Victor Pickridge (Puck) at Kuala Krau. Puck wanted to join the expedition and volunteered to arrange all sampans boats and guides.

I can't stress enough what an eccentric fellow this 'Puck' was. Talk about the 'madness of empire' – Puck was it! From what I can gather his wife, Mollie, was much the same. I have been shown a book that mentions Puck and his wife and describes how they did their daily rounds of the estate during the Emergency. An extract from the book states that: 'Each morning Mollie insisted on going on the rounds with Puck, for she hated the idea of being left alone. Mollie held the gun, Puck drove the Land Rover – with his hat on the seat filled with grenades. Yet Mollie remembers it now as "a wonderful life, although the CTs fired guns every night and there were so many bullet holes in the roof when it rained it was like living in a colander." The same book also says of Puck, "He was determined to be 'British' with a capital 'B' and as the CTs stepped up their attacks, he decided it was time to show the flag – literally.

Every evening at sundown, he lined up his squad of home-trained guards beside the flagstaff. Ceremoniously, the Union Jack was hauled down for the night while 'Puck' blew his own home-made trumpet." I never witnessed any of this and nothing like this ever went on with Scottish Malayan, but having met Puck, I can well believe it. Being a Scot I would definitely say Puck was determined to be 'English' with a capital 'E'. I had never met anyone like him before and have never since. He was totally fearless, almost to the point of insanity. The flag hoisting may have been true – having met him, it's very possible. I saw him for the first time in 1955, when Malaya was nearing independence. Puck in his day held many positions. Before the war he was a rubber planter and was in the Malayan Straits Volunteers when the Japanese invaded. He was said to be the last man to escape from mainland Malaya. In a sampong and all alone, he landed in Ceylon some weeks later. There he joined Force 136 and went back into Malaya during the Japanese occupation to help train Chinese Guerrillas for the Malayan Underground. He knew most of the high-ranking guerrillas in the Malayan People's Anti-British Army, as they were once his comrades fighting the Japanese. Puck had many a tale to tell.

The difference between this conflict and most other wars, as it appeared to me then, was that the CTs were fighting a cause, whereas the planters were fighting for their lives. It's hard to explain the various emotions one feels in that predicament. During the war I was in Palestine and although there was a great deal of danger I was with my pals – Scots, Liverpudlians, Cockneys and Welsh. It gave us all a strength of heart, courage and a feeling of security knowing that you are with your countrymen and comrades, looking out for one another. In a foreign land, a long way from home, isolated, in a situation where your fellows speak a foreign language and may desert at any time, fighting an enemy you seldom see, with the chance that you may be shot in the back at any given moment, it's a very different matter! One becomes extremely alert, with an attitude of readiness, capable of executing anything or anyone that makes a wrong move. On looking back now, I believe the company directors back home in Edinburgh were aware of this when hiring four Gurkhas as our personal bodyguards. They are well known for their loyalty and courage.

Anyway back to the expedition. We met at Kuala Krau early on a Saturday morning in May 1953, having walked up the railway track from Sungai Tekal, a distance of five miles. Puck was waiting on the quay with his personal bodyguards – five Malays armed with shotguns, grenades and parongs, a wild looking lot! Dodd had his escort of four Malay SP and I had my escort of four Malays and two Gurkhas. After introductions, we all piled into the waiting sampans and set off down the Sungai Pahang to a landing point a guide had selected, it being the nearest point to Bukit Hantu (Ghost Hill), which was some two miles distant. The walk through dense jungle to the caves was rough going, everyone was pestered with leeches, especially Dodd as he was wearing shorts.

Arriving at Bukit Hantu, we all stopped and looked up in amazement. The limestone hill rose vertically in front of us and, still more amazing, when we got inside it was completely hollow. In one place a ray of sunlight, forming an aperture in the roof, was shining on the wall of the cave making it look like a giant cinema screen. Puck went up to it and wrote 'Puck was here 1955'. I wonder if it is still there? The floor of the cave was literally moving with insects of all sorts and sizes. Huge iguana lizards were darting here and there, feeding on dead bats which had fallen from the roof. There must have been thousands of tons of bat guano in this one cave alone. We took samples of the guano and then made for home. What surprised me most was that the two Gurkhas had refused to go inside the caves, having been told they were haunted. The Gurkhas were always so fearless, but it seems there was one thing they were afraid of – ghosts!

On the way back upriver we were suddenly attacked and shot at by CT. We had to take cover on the opposite bank. However, no one was hit and after a short time we proceeded upstream to Kuala Krau. Following the long walk home, we gave our thanks and farewell to Puck and his party. The samples of guano were sent to the ICI and Malayan fertilizers in KL for analysis. The reports received back from both these organisations were very good indeed. So mining rights were applied for and granted. Unfortunately, these were put on hold by Jock Neill. Once again he seemed to have it in for us!

Kristnan Menon and Menachie

Having a good clerk was an asset, one that was good at figures was an additional bonus. A clerk of this standing was hard to come by and to find one to take up residence at Sungai Tekal was difficult, especially during the Emergency. With a labour force of around 200 and their dependents to account for, it was no simple task. The monthly accounts had to be completed by the 15th of the current month and sent to the board of directors in Edinburgh by the 23rd for scrutiny. Any irregularities, such as overspending or underspending, had to be accounted for and explained in detail. So a good clerk was a must.

Two weeks after my taking over the estate, the clerk left due to CT threats and intimidation. He and his family were housed in the assistant's bungalow and had left in a hurry, leaving behind a collection of lizards and snakes in large glass jars preserved in alcohol (meths). The collection had been started by one of the previous assistant managers. The position for a clerk was advertised without success for several weeks. The money was very good but the isolation of the estate, together with CT activity in the district was a stumbling block. When things got desperate my next door neighbour (five miles down the railway track) Archie Campbell suggested that I contact a Chinese Accountancy agency in Kuala Lumpur as the agency ran a clerk hire service. So I did, and the agency sent me Kristnan Menon, a Madras Indian. Menon was a graduate of Madras University and a qualified accountant. He was very effective in the office and thereafter Sungai Tekal was always the first in the group to have their accounts completed and posted to Edinburgh. In addition, he would answer all minor correspondence with ease. A very handy man to have around indeed. Unfortunately he had a drink problem and his employment with the agency was only temporary. One day he received an offer from a tin mining company to run their accounts dept. This would give him a much better salary. He told me he liked working on Sungai Tekal and gave me the opportunity to offer him more money, which I did. This was a good deal for both of us, as the salary I offered him was less than I had been paying the agency. Menon was married with two children and his son had just qualified as a doctor in Kuala Lumpur and his daughter was now studying law.

When Menon took the full-time post, he sent for his wife. I knew he was drinking heavily and I thought that, with the arrival of his wife, he would ease up on the drink. His drinking habits were odd. He would work continuously to finish the accounts and get all other work up to date, then he would go off on a binge for two to three days. For the last few days of the month there was little to do, as all his work had been neatly completed before going off on his drinking binge. Without drink he seemed to become melancholy. The other odd thing about Menon was that he had ten fingers, two thumbs, and twelve toes.

With the arrival of his wife, his drinking habits changed. Instead of drinking in the bungalow, he started drinking at the toddy shop and then at the café/shop where he fell under the spell of Menachie, an attractive Tamil woman. It was said she had a provocative look and the workers called her 'evil eye'. They also believed she could cast spells and she certainly did over Menon! Menachie was the wife of the engine driver, Ramaswang. An engine driver was similar to a marine engineer, he looked after the steam engine which drove the oil palm factory and was responsible for the maintenance and running of the factory. Menachie sent her husband mad, but that is another story. Menon's drink problem and his fascination for Menachie, caused his own wife to leave him and return to Kuala Lumpur. Even with all these problems around him, his work never suffered and was always up to scratch. The old assistant's bungalow where he lived was some 200 yards behind my bungalow. At night we could hear him wailing and calling out for Menachie. On several occasions the guards were sent over to see if they could help, but he sent them back saying, "I am now in the hands of my ancestors!" What that meant, I never got to know. He was in a very bad way. Having discussed the matter with the dresser who, like Menon, was from the Madras district, we thought it was best to leave him alone and hope that he would recover given time.

The following week Mac Hunter visited the estate to make his monthly report. In late afternoon he decided to visit the labour lines. Being fluent in Tamil, he chatted with several of the workers. My Tamil had improved by this stage but I wasn't fluent yet. When we got to the café, we found Menon slumped over a table, clutching an almost empty bottle of illicit Chinese sam sue (rice whisky). The Chinese manager was most apologetic and said he had come in and mixed the liquor with his coffee. Menon was carried back to the bungalow by two friends from the café. The next morning he was back at work at 7 a.m. as if nothing had happened. He could not remember being in the café or seeing Hunter the previous afternoon. Hunter gave him a severe dressing down and told him he was barred from the toddy shop and café. In private, Mac told me to look for another clerk. He did offer to send up his own private secretary, Raja Gobeill, as a stopgap. Raja was known to be jealous of Kristnan Menon's skill and popularity. The next month, when

Menon had finished his monthly accounts and was up to date with all other work, he went missing for three days. His bungalow servant had reported that he had been drinking heavily and I presumed that he had obtained some illicit sam sue again. On the fourth day of his absence I had decided to pay him a visit. As I entered the bungalow there was a strong smell of sickly sweet incense, mixed with camphor. Then I saw an uncanny sight. Menon was sitting bolt upright in a sort of home-made shrine on a Sedan-type, rattan chair, surrounded by withering flowers, clutching a large photo of Menachie. In his left hand he held a mug and by his side was a large glass jar, at the bottom of which were the remains of a lizard. He had been drinking the methylated spirits from the jars of embalmed reptiles. I tried to speak to him but he gave no response – for a moment I thought he was dead! The dresser was sent for. He also tried to wake him but failed. When the dresser first approached Menon, he was unsure and appeared to be afraid of something. I suggested we move Menon down to the estate hospital, where the dresser and his assistant could keep an eye on him. The four Malay escorts and two Gurkhas were uneasy and somewhat reluctant to assist in lifting Menon on to the stretcher. One of the Malay police asked to be excused, stating that his wife was pregnant and he did not want to look at the man with twelve fingers and twelve toes, as this could have a bad effect on his expected baby. In those days Malays believed that when a woman became pregnant all ugly images should be removed from view. Looking at something grotesque was thought to frighten the unborn child and could mark the baby. Her husband would also avoid looking at anything ugly or deformed.

The dresser and the Gurkhas thought that Menon was in some sort of trance with his ancestors and did not want to wake him. They also believed his twelve fingers and toes gave him special powers, enabling him to take revenge on them if they woke him. Was Menon in a trance or under one of Menachie's spells or just dead drunk, perhaps all three? One will never know. It took Menon four days to recover, during which time I spoke to his doctor son in Kuala Lumpur. He knew about his father's problems and had made arrangements for him to be taken to Tanjong Rambutan Mental Hospital. That was the last I heard of Kristnan Menon. I was sorry to see him go, he had been a great help in many ways. Mac Hunter did send up a clerk but not his private secretary. As for the beguiling Menachie, she continued to cast her spells and create havoc.

Spells

On the subject of spells causing harm and bewilderment, one such spell befell a Scottish family.

One of Scottish Malayan managers was Victor Kinloch, the youngest son of a late Colonel Kinloch of Kinloch Estate, Meigle. Their family crypt was at a place called Roundy Hill, close by the Glamis Road in Kirriemuir. As boys it was an adventure for us to go down into the old moat, climb over the high wall, enter the grounds and look through the iron gates into the crypt, whilst keeping a look out for the gamekeeper 'Clerkie'.

Victor's father served with the army in India for several years. It was said that during a tour of duty on the Malabar Coast he took an idol from an old Hindu temple and was asked by the local Tamil guru to replace it. This he ignored, also taking no heed of a spell and warning given by the guru. He took the idol back to Scotland and in doing so activated the holy man's curse on the Kinloch family. He placed the idol on the first landing of the staircase in Kinloch House, facing north. This in itself was bad luck! During this period the Great War broke out, the colonel's eldest sons were killed within months of volunteering. The old colonel lost interest in life, was invalided out of the army and died shortly afterwards – some say of a broken heart – leaving Kinloch Estate almost bankrupt, or so the story goes.

After the war Victor joined Scottish Malayan Estates and went out to Malaya with his wife and young family and was quickly promoted to general manager. He sent every penny home, hoping to revive Kinloch Estate. Whilst in Malay his three children died and soon after, his wife also died. The Kinloch Estate was now in the hands of the receivers. Victor went home a sick man and when the estate finally went bankrupt it is said he also died of a broken heart.

The saga continues – the day before the contents of Kinloch House were auctioned off, two Tamil Indians were seen viewing the contents and thereafter the idol disappeared. This, I believe, was in the late twenties or early thirties. In those days, it was most unusual to see Tamil Indians in the Scottish countryside. The last I heard of the Kinloch family was when a friend of ours George McLaren, a farmer of Bankhead of Kinloch, bought Kinloch House in the early sixties and made it into a hotel. One of the others interested in the sale was a George Kinloch, a bachelor living in London and a relative of Victor Kinloch. Was the idol restored to its rightful place in the old temple on the Malabar Coast, thus ending the curse? In any case it was too late for the Kinloch family. According to myth, before putting a Tamil curse on a person or family, a clay image of them would be made with a hair from each individual embedded in his or her image. Could this have been possible with the Kinloch family? Perhaps the Tamil gurus had other methods of casting a curse. What I do know, is that Tamil plantation workers went to extreme ends when casting spells and in most cases, sorry to say, it worked, with sometimes tragic effect.

The Tamil Syndicate, Manachie and Ramasamy

The Tamils had a unique system for financing personal loans for weddings, funeral and such like, which was very complicated. Tamils of the same financial status formed a syndicate, putting into an account one month's salary each, say $100. This was done by one person paying in his monthly salary of $100 and the other nine members would support him and his family for that month and so on until each member had paid in $100 making a total of $1,000. A member of the syndicate could borrow up to $200 for some important family event. The loan having been approved by the other nine members of the syndicate with the proviso that the loan would be paid back, in full, within ten months, plus a 10% interest charge.

In certain circumstances the syndicate would lend money to an outsider but in that case the interest rate would be between 15% and 20%, with a payback period of six months. All outsiders had to have a guarantor with ready cash before the loan would be granted.

Overall the syndicate could make a yearly profit of around $200 on interest payments, that is if nothing went wrong! This profit would be shared out between the syndicate members, provided that they were not in debt to the syndicate at the time of the share out. If a member was in debt to the syndicate during this period, only a percentage of the share out would be paid to them. Therefore, members who had not borrowed during this period, received the largest share. Very complex and most difficult to figure out. The share out would involve some long and fiery disputes that would go on for days. The only good thing about it was that it never came to blows. It was something no sensible estate manager would get involved in, even if asked to give a judgement.

One of the outsiders who was given a loan of $250 was 'spellbinding' Menachie. She convinced the members of the syndicate that her need was great, in the pretence that her niece was getting married, on a neighbouring estate. How she managed to obtain this loan is difficult to figure out, as her engine driver husband Ramasamy knew nothing about it. Having received the cash, Menachie left the next morning on the train to Mentakab without telling anyone. The next day her husband was not at work. Around midday he came into the office in a shocking state, carrying three pieces of tin foil with Tamil writing on them. One he had found in his rice bowl, another in his bed and the third on the back of his front door. From what I could gather, this meant he would be without food, rest and shelter. Ramasamy could give no reason for this, only that his wife had put them there and had disappeared. Being an engine driver he was a man of some standing. In 1946 he had gone back to India to marry Menachie. It was an arranged marriage. During their married life together Ramasamy had bedecked her with gold which she seemingly enjoyed flaunting. The gold may have been the reason she was able to borrow $250 from the syndicate.

With each passing day Ramasamy's condition deteriorated. All he could think and talk about was Menachie and the sorcery contained in the charms she had left behind. Whatever it was, it was making him a very sick man and moreover I was afraid for his safety. An oil palm factory is not the safest place to be if you are in poor health. Accidents began to happen. He forgot to open the outlet valve on the dual filter for the estate water supply. The pressure from the water pump built up in the filter and blew the concave bottom out to convex. The final straw came when two 44 gallon drums of oil palm sludge exploded. He had overfilled the drums and had not left them to settle. This oil palm sludge was used in the making of cow cake amongst other things. After these episodes it was necessary to lay Ramasamy off and to find him some sort of treatment. The Chinese fitter suggested he would melt down strips of tin foil with his welding set or for Ramasamy himself to melt the strips down, in the furnace of the steam boiler. Perhaps this would break the spell. Ramasamy would not agree to this, fearing something worse would happen to him. He became very thin and wandered around the estate in a daze.

Menachie on the other hand had opened a small Indian health shop in Temerloh, selling all kinds of Indian medicines, remedies, love potions and charms, with all the necessary advice on how to administer them. She was seen walking about with a tall handsome

Tamil man. It was said that he was the lover she had run away with in India, before her wedding to Ramasamy, and that she had sent money to India for his passage to Malaya. Ramasamy was a committee member of the estate film club and his fellow members strongly recommended he should pay off Menachie's loan, which he did. This was a good move, thereafter he began to regain his strength and to get his sanity back. He did come back to work but, sorry to say, he was not the same man. Why Menachie put a spell on him in the first place, we will never know. And we will never know if she withdrew the spell having found her lover. The less said about superstition the better. This includes spells and black magic.

CHAPTER 14

Meeting the Orang Asli

Dusty Miller

Most of the police officers in charge of the plantation SP were ex-Palestine police sergeants. The British mandate of Palestine ended in May 1948. The following year, they were all promoted to the rank of Police Lieutenant. Owing to the amount of CT activity and the remoteness of the plantations in this part of the state of Pahang, the officers in charge of the SP forces only did a short tour of duty – four months. One of those officers was an ex-RAF Flight Lieutenant named Miller and as usual, like all Millers at that time, known as 'Dusty'. I never did get to know his true first name. Dusty was from Kirkintilloch and during the war was an Air gunner in the RAF. He had done four tours of duty of 36 flights in each, mainly over Germany. This was most unusual as many air gunners were either killed or wounded on their first tour of duty. Dusty's luck was still holding out as he had been caught up in several CT ambushes, in which some of his comrades were killed. He would visit the estate once or twice a week to inspect the Malay Specials and to solve any problems, which were many.

On one occasion he had a young Malay Police Inspector newly out from Police College with him. Dusty was given the task of showing him the ropes and to help him with his English. On this occasion, I picked Dusty and the young inspector up at the Sungai Tekal Halt. On the way back to the bungalow we passed the labour line and a row of toilets nearby. Dusty pointed to the toilets and said to the young inspector, "That is a shit house" and with a look of approval the inspector said in return, "That is a shit house." Dusty answered, "Very good." When we arrived at the bungalow they were asked in for coffee. Dusty pointed to a chair and said as he sat down, "I sit on my arse," and the young inspector repeated, "I sit on my arse." At this point I asked Dusty to let up as I did not want to be involved in this charade. The inspector was very young and I thought it was in very bad taste.

As I have mentioned before we were led to believe there were three major 'taboos' that can lead to an immediate volatile reaction from a Malay – insult his wife, his religion, or make him look a fool. The word for this is 'amok' which is a Malay word. I have seen the aftermath of the 'amok' and it is not pretty. The Malays were permitted by law to carry their kriss or parong (sword/dagger) This may be why the 'amok' could be so violent.

However, several weeks later the young Malay inspector took over command of an outlying police post, some miles from Kuala Krau. When the local Chief of Police, Jock Neill, in full uniform, complete with swagger stick, visited the post for the first time, the young inspector gave him a smart salute and pulled up a chair for him and said, "Sit on your arse, Sir." Jock was not amused and asked the inspector who taught him to speak that way. The inspector replied, "Lieutenant Miller, Sir." Dusty was given a severe reprimand and ordered to make an apology to the young inspector. Dusty was immediately transferred and I never saw him again. Things that appeared trivial, could end with serious consequences.

A Gift From Teck Seng

It was Christmas 1954 on Sungai Tekal when I received a present – a case of 48 small jars of caviar from a Chinese merchant and dear friend, Chop Teck Seng of Mentakab. At that time Scottish Malayan estate managers were applying for an increase in their cost of living allowance, due to rising prices in Malaya. I had never tasted caviar, however our Tamil cook knew all about it, having cooked for the District Officer. He suggested we have it on toast with afternoon tea. Over time I began to like the caviar and so did my assistant Dodd. We decided to buy another case and Dodd agreed to pay a third of the price. During the caviar period, Mac Hunter paid us a routine visit and the high cost of living was discussed, the company having agreed to increase the cost of living allowance. That afternoon when the cook served up caviar on toast, Mac Hunter shouted, "What the hell is this, the trouble with you lot is not the high cost of living but the cost of high living." Once I had explained the circumstances of how this came about, he laughed exclaiming, "There is one thing for certain, you can always be sure of the unexpected when you visit Sungai Tekal."

Meeting the Orang Asli

When I met Jimmy Baxter on Sungai Tekal back in April 1948 he prepared me for the occasional visit from the Orang Asli (Aborigines). He gave me some insight into their ways. This stood me in good stead when I eventually met them. Known locally as Orang Liar (Orang – human; Liar – shy, unbroken, undomesticated), they were a nomadic tribe that roamed the jungle, living off fruit and game. Experts with their 10 foot blow pipes and 'ipoh upus' (poison dart) they could kill a monkey at 50 yards. Monkeys were part of their staple diet. They wore very little clothing, if any, and lived in and from the jungle.

Postcard I purchased in Malaya of two Orang Asli

My first encounter with them was several weeks after I took over from Jimmy. I had just finished dinner and was sitting on the veranda engrossed in learning the Tamil language, but being pestered by insects attracted by the tilly lamps we used, as there was no electric light. Just at that moment, two Orang Asli strolled onto

121

the veranda and sat down. Unbeknown to me Middleton, my manager, had employed a tribe of Aboriginies to cut jungle timber. The two men helped themselves to the cigarettes on the table and spoke to me in a language/dialect I had not heard before. They pointed to various items, babbling on as they inspected them. When they had almost finished their cigarettes, which they had drawn on until red-hot, one of them opened his mouth and pushed the red-hot butt into a rotten back tooth. He stood with his mouth wide open while his companion also rammed his cigarette end into the bad tooth. They appeared to contemplate this for some time before walking through into the kitchen, where the Chinese cook gave them some cheese and bread. They then went out into the garden, had a look around, picked up their blow-pipes and left having taken just what they needed at the time and no more. Believing everything was there for the taking, they did not comprehend what stealing was.

Now and then a tribe would visit the estate and ask for work, their speciality was cutting jungle timber. This type of work was always available to them as we required a constant supply of wood for the rubber smokehouses and jungle timber for fence posts. A sample of the timber required was given and a price agreed for each item. They counted on their fingers, therefore the cut timber would be stacked in layers of five and ten high. Each pile would be counted and paid for individually. The tribe would make camp where they were cutting the timber, working for three or four days only, then moving on, returning nine to twelve months later.

The tribe had several special camp sites in the jungle, mainly by a river, where they would hold their rituals. They had an interesting way of resolving any issues. The men would sit round the fire discussing any problems and would then fall asleep around the dying embers to dream. The answer would come to one of them and this would be the solution to the problem, come what may.

One of their special sites was a beauty spot close to the Bentong–Kuala Lumpur road, near the Genting Highlands on the Sungai Benus (Benus river). Before WW1 a rubber planter named Huston met his death at this ritual site in mysterious circumstances. Huston was a planter manager on an estate near Bentong. He had employed a tribe to help cut out part of the jungle for a rubber planting agenda. Attracted to one of the young women, he kept her at his bungalow after her tribe had moved on. She told him of this beautiful site near the Genting Highlands, to which he made a visit.

He was most impressed by the landscape and as the site was reasonably close to the main Bentong road, he decided to apply for permission to build a hotel and rest centre for Europeans. Permission was given together with a long lease. He formed a syndicate with some of his friends. A shelter-cum-office was erected on the site, so he could supervise the work that was due to commence.

Finding a shelter on the edge of their sacred ground, angered the Orang Asli who had come there for a spiritual ritual. So true to tradition, that night the men discussed the problem, fell asleep round the fire to dream for a solution. It just so happened that when the Aboriginies arrived on site that afternoon Huston and his Orang Asli woman were staying in the shelter awaiting the arrival of two investors to view the project. They had been drinking heavily all day. That night, after his partners left, Huston continued to drink alone. His Aboriginal woman had gone to the tribe's camp to visit some of her relatives.

On her return she told Huston that the tribe was angry at what had taken place and the men of the tribe were now asleep dreaming for a solution. Huston dismissed this as ignorant foolery and kept on drinking. In the early hours of the morning Huston woke up from a drunken dream, shouting in Malay "rimau, rimau" that he was being chased by a tiger.

The Orang Asli men were discussing the outcome of the judicial dream, which was that Huston would fall over a cliff and be drowned. On hearing Huston shouting, "rimau, rimau" the Orang Asli men came running to help, shouting and banging on tin cans in order to scare off the tiger. Huston, thinking they were after him, ran up a nearby mound and fell over a small cliff into the river Sungai Benus and true to the Orang Asli dream was drowned. The coroner's verdict was death by misadventure. How true! Thereafter the other investors got cold feet and the development project was abandoned. I wonder why? The Sakai still hold their ritual on site, at least they were still doing so when I left Malaya in 56.

This is a cutting I took from the Malay Times 1952.
Awang anak Rawang, an Aborigine from Sarawak, won the George
Cross serving with the Security Forces "for coolness, fortitude and
offensive spirit of the highest order".

Almost!

Very few people are remembered by the good deeds they have done,
it is always the bad and silly things that come to mind. For instance,
if you are talking about a fellow and mention the good deeds he has
done, no one will remember him, but if you then say he got drunk
one night, smashed his car and was arrested, everyone will instantly
recognise him! That's life.

Well a similar thing happened to me, this is from a planter's point of view:

It happened during the yearly manuring program of the oil palm division on Sungai Tekal Estate. The programme was over some 500 acres of the youngest palms, each palm was to be given an application of ¾lb of Christmas Island Rock Phosphate in ten pockets around the palm, six ounces in each pocket at six feet from the palm base. At the same time as the manuring programme was due to commence, a building contract was given out to a Chinese building contractor Foo Ah Toon for the construction of new labour lines and a new police canteen.

At this point in time I was due my six days' local leave, which was a must in the eyes of the company, and as usual I was to fly to Penang. Before leaving the plantation, I gave instruction to the head kanganies to offload the rock phosphate, which was due to arrive sometime during my absence and to start the manuring programme, all very straightforward.

Two railway wagons duly arrived and were shunted off by hand into the Sungia Tekal siding. The first wagon containing rock phosphate was unloaded and taken to the store. The contents of the second wagon were distributed throughout the oil palm area, in order to start the first stage of the manuring programme. However, unknown to the head kanganies, this was cement ordered by the Chinese building contractor. Both the rock phosphate and the cement were in gunny bags and both looked the same in colour and texture. Fortunately the blunder was discovered by my assistant Dodd before the actual application took place and all the cement was recovered and taken to the building site.

At this stage of his training Dodd had taken over the running of the rubber division (Sungai Chang Estate) and was fully employed in this task. He was also briefed on what was taking place on the oil palm division and that the head kanganies in charge of the division would call on him should there be any irregularity.

It was only when the Chinese building contractor Foo Ah Toon pointed out to Dodd that one of the empty wagons at Sungia Tekal Halt contained cement and this wagon had been booked to him, that the day was saved! By nightfall of that day, news of what could have been a calamity had flashed to all Scottish Malayan Estate managers. By the time I got back from local leave the current rumour was such that I had manured all oil palms on Sungai Tekal with cement, some 2,200 acres in all, this was being said by planters throughout the state of Pahang. When asked about it, there was no good in trying to explain what actually happened, all I could do was laugh with the jokers and hope that the event would soon blow over. As time goes by there are many things in life that befall you, over which you have no control, and this was just one of them. I must say that this event did create some amusement and I did take quite a lot of stick over it. However it was not as bad as what happened to a friend and fellow planter, Major Dickie Dickson. Dickie had taken over a large estate near Seremban and was giving a dinner party to celebrate his good fortune. During dinner, CT attacked the bungalow and while Dickie was strapping on his revolver the gun went off and he shot himself in the foot. Several weeks later he gave a curry tiffin and while demonstrating to guests how he shot himself in the foot the gun went off again and this time blew off part of his big toe! Knowing Dickie, no doubt drink was involved in both cases. He also took a lot of stick over it.

CHAPTER 15
Home Leave and Half Cut

I was now making arrangements for my six months' leave and was booked first class (all travel and hotel accommodation was first class for Scottish Malayan Estate managers) on the *Southern Cross*, a new cruise liner on a round world cruise. I was to join the ship in Singapore, sailing to Australia through the Panama Canal and on to Southampton. Unfortunately my father fell ill, the cruise was cancelled and I flew home with BOAC.

In those days it was a three-day trip with an overnight stop in Ceylon at the Mount Lavinia Hotel and a four-hour lunch stop in Rome. A good lunch and a few beers was had in the airport restaurant. I was badly in need of a hair cut as it had grown fairly long and curly. With time on my hands and as I had not had a shave for almost three days, I found the airport barbers. The barber shop was busy and I had to wait my turn.

When called, I was given a good shave by a women barber and then set upon by two other women – one, a manicurist, attended to my hands and nails while the other female barber began cutting my hair. She had almost finished when the stewardess walked in and told me to come at once to join the flight. Seemingly the flight controller had been calling for me over the tannoy. I left the salon half cut!

By the time I arrived in London all the barbers' shops were closed. I caught the late night sleeper train to Aberdeen. In the carriage with me were three well-dressed city gentlemen with bowler hats reading newspapers or doing crosswords. They were giving me the occasional side glance, so to satisfy their curiosity I explained that I had half a hair cut in Rome and was to have the other half in Kirriemuir. When I finally got home, the local barber Danny McGregor was my first port of call. Dan was in my class at school. There was a warm welcome. Dan's price list was on the wall, tariffs being: Shave 1/- (one shilling or 12d – 5p in today's money); Hair cut 9d; Trim 6d and so on. When I asked Dan for half a hair cut at 4½ pennies, Dan said, "There's nae half cuts here," and pointed to the tariffs, "but seeing it's yooz yourself, Dykes, I'll gie ye a half cut." Willie Mill the local reporter got to hear about it and I believe there was a write-up in the local weekly free paper.

Joe Monro, the local second-hand car dealer, came down to see me and I was inveigled into buying a car from him. Joe was a big way in second-hand cars and known nationwide at the time. I was offered a good deal by Joe, if all had gone as agreed, but that is another story. The car I bought was a Humber Hawk, one year old, 16,000 miles on the clock, and one owner who was P.S. Bile the accountant who signed all the English bank notes at that time. A beautiful car.

Six months' home leave with SME was on full pay, the only requirement was that I should attend two directors' board meetings in Edinburgh. One when I arrived home, the other before going back to Malaya. These were great days and home leave was indeed a joy. Having completed my contract with SME, three and a half years as manager of Sungai Tekal Estate I had earned six months' home leave. Leave was from 18th June 1955 to 2nd January 1956, the best possible time to be at home taking in all the summer attractions and Christmas.

A Gift From the Labour Force

Before I left Sungai Tekal for six months' home leave, the Tamil labour force and the Chinese sub-contractor labourers gave me a curry tiffin farewell soirée. A grand affair, on the last afternoon before my departure. The Malay SP guards had said their 'selamat jalan' (bon voyage) the previous afternoon in their own unique way. As usual the Tamil curry was served up on banana leaves with all the usual sambals (spicy condiments/relishes). After several speeches, as a mark of appreciation, I was presented with a gift from the labour force. A £100 Harrods voucher, a great deal of money in 1955, which was a most unusual gesture in more ways than one, as the average daily wage for a Tamil plantation worker was only $2.50 (30 pence) a day. I was overwhelmed by their generosity and looking back, I think the labour force felt I had done the best I could for them. Their loyalty may have gone some way to saving my life. Anyway, it was an unprecedented gesture and one I will never forget.

To spend this voucher I had to go in person to Harrods in London. Kirriemuir to London was a two-day journey – no motorways in those days. At that time it just so happened that an old friend, George Cargill, was home in Kirrie on holiday from Canada and had a car to pick up in London. It was arranged that he would drive down to London with me and share the fuel bill.

Before his call-up for RAF war service in 1941, George was a radio engineer and electrician with Hosie Electrical Engineers in Kirrie and Forfar. When I was serving my time there as an electrician/radio engineer, George was a qualified engineer and taught me a lot. With his help I did a postal course on radio engineering with Murphy Radios, qualifying in 1940. When we arrived in London, I dropped George at his destination and went on to Harrods, with the £100 voucher. I smoked in those days and my plan was to buy 50 cigarettes and get the change in hard cash. To my disappointment I got the change in vouchers and not knowing what to buy left me in a quandary. I bought a very expensive trench coat, the height of fashion of the day; a Harrods tweed sport jacket; and the balance of the voucher was spent on presents for family and friends. Harrods parcelled up all the purchases in their special way for me to collect later. I spent the night in London and called back for the goods the following morning.

On the way home, near Mansfield the car developed a whining noise coming from the back. I stopped but could see nothing that would cause this and continued my journey. Eventually the noise got so loud that I was stopped by the police and directed to the nearest Humber garage, which was in Mansfield. According to the motor mechanic, the trouble was the back axle differential. Seemingly it had been filled with the wrong oil. A new differential was required and the work would take two days. I booked in at the nearest hotel which was the Green Dragon, a pleasant cheery place with good food and beer. While playing dominos I met a Major who was a member of Club Pasha Staff in the famous Arab Legion, a mounted camel regiment stationed in Jordan. We had a lot in common regarding the Palestine mandate. I enjoyed my short stay there.

The car was ready on the third day, delayed, as the garage had to send away for a new differential. Joe Monroe, the Kirrie car dealer from whom the car was purchased, duly paid the total repair bill, just not the hotel expenses. I arrived home the following day.

It was now mid-summer and all the holiday attractions were in place, the main venue being the Highland Games. I had again palled up with an old crony and school friend 'Gaffer' Norman Campbell. Gaffer had done well in the timber business and was now a large merchant with his own saw-mills. He had served with Argyll and Southern Highlanders during the war and still wore his kilt most of the time. He was a keen follower of the Highland Games and had tried his hand at tossing the caber, throwing the hammer and wrestling, and he liked a drink like many of us. During that lovely summer we went to most Highland Games and gatherings taking place throughout Scotland. The finals at Braemar in early September was and still is a great sporting event, together with a regal gathering of all tartans and many pipe bands. Later in the year the Edinburgh Tattoo was another great event.

Most Sundays were spent fishing on the River Esk at Justinhaugh and late in the afternoon we would have 'high tea' in the Justinhaugh Hotel. The proprietor Mary Ferrier was always pleased to see us and made us most welcome. Mary was known far and wide for her Sunday night ceilidhs which included some 'bothy' ballads and 'corn kisters'. The ceilidhs were boisterous affairs and when the ranting got too much, Mary would come in and shout, "One more hooch and you're 'a' oot," and she meant it. This was Sunday in Scotland and in those days all public bars were closed, you were only given a drink if you were a traveller having a meal – a harsh law that had to be upheld! To overcome this restriction Mary had 'special' sandwiches on the tables for everyone to see, brave be the person who dare eat them! One of the singers was Hunt Young, the gamekeeper for Sir Harry Hope of Kinnettles Estate at Douglastown in the Forfar Glamis Road. Hunt was good company and I had many a good shoot with him on the estate. His grandfather Blindie Young was head gamekeeper on the Glamis Estate for the Bowes Lyons and knew the late Queen Mother in her younger days.

Meeting Della Again

Early in the evening of Saturday 7th August 1955 (a day I will never forget) I was getting ready to go out for the evening. I was in the scullery of my parents' house – 'The Dumpling' – stripped to the waist, washing down at one of the deep sinks below the window. When I looked up, Della was at the garden gate. She was beautiful, and with that first glance I was intoxicated by her. It was eleven years since I had seen her and she was even more lovely than I remembered. I know not how to explain it, but at that moment I fell in love. To see Della was to love her, love but her and love forever. That night we went out together and reminisced about our teenage years. We visited some of the old haunts we used to frequent, ending up at the Saturday night dance in Kirrie Town Hall.

Della and I by the river Esk 1955

The next morning I called upon Meg and Doug Herd, the parents of my best friend Angus who had been killed in the war. Della was visiting them whilst on holiday with her sister Mary in Dundee. It was a beautiful sunny day and we decided to go out and make the best of it. We drove to the top of Glen Esk and stopped for high tea in the hotel there. On the way home we called in at the Justinhaugh Hotel and joined in the fun, singing bothy ballads and listening to Scottish Country music. The merrymaking went on well past midnight. We had a very pleasant day indeed. Over the next days the weather remained glorious and Della and I made the best of it, visiting many local attractions. During these few days Della and I fell in love. Without her I knew I could never again be happy. What a glorious summer we had!

All too soon, it was December and my home leave was almost over, it was amazing how quickly the months had passed, my enjoyment was coming to an end. It was time to 'yoke' again. At my last meeting with the directors of SME in Edinburgh, I had accepted the post as manager of Sungai Buloh Estate with a handsome increase in salary on a three-year contract. Seeing family and old friends was a breath of fresh air, but parting and bidding farewell to Della was a sombre task. On previous occasions when I had left to go overseas, I had been excited and full of anticipation for what lay ahead. This time I was dispirited and lonely and, to add to this, it was Hogmanay. I was booked to fly back to Malaya on 31st December. Once there I was to make arrangements for Della to join me. But fate had other plans for us.

CHAPTER 16
Back to Malaya

I flew first to Rome with BOAC where we had brunch and refuelled and from there on to Ceylon for an overnight stop. I was booked into the luxurious Mount Lavinia Hotel which stood on cliffs above a beautiful sandy beach. The next day I flew into Penang where I got off and booked the ferry and night train to Kuala Lumpur. Penang had a railway station, but no trains! One had to book at the railway station but take the ferry to Butterworth on the Malayan mainland and board the night train there.

The next morning I was back on Sangai Buloh Estate, Sandy Tosh, the outgoing manager, had sent the estate car to meet my early morning train from Butterworth. The takeover of the estate was a simple process as I had been there in 1950 as an assistant under the General Manager, Mac Hunter.

The next time I would meet Sandy Tosh was some years later when he and his Siamese wife, Cheloom, took up a smallholding at Slade Gardens in Kirriemuir. In the 1960s when I started Angus Foods, a canning factory in Brechin, I employed Sandy as Season Liaison Officer (troubleshooter) between the factory and fruit growers. He did well and enjoyed the job. My daughter Ann and her friend Audrey were very fond of Cheloom and made regular visits to her home which was full of the unusual aroma of drying herbs. Cheloom cooked them traditional Thai food. They also enjoyed her mystical Siamese stories and unique delicate manner.

With Malayan Independence due the following year (1957), new legislation was pending. The day of the 'White Rubber Planter' was coming to and end. Rubber and palm oil estates were to be barred from taking on European assistants. Therefore it came as no surprise to be told that Sungai Buloh was up for sale. I was directed to conduct and execute a sale as quickly as possible. Following the sale I was to take up the billet as manager of Strathairlie Estate. Sungai Buloh was finally sold to a Chinese syndicate. The incoming manager could not speak English, so the transfer of the estate was done in Malay, a language we were both fluent in. He stayed with me for two weeks during the takeover period.

Before leaving Sungai Buloh the new manager said that the new owners wished me to dine with them at the Buket Bintang Hotel (Hill Star Hotel) in Kula Lumpur. This hotel was known to be a brothel and very few Europeans dined there. I was surprised and enquired as to whether he had the name correct. He assured me he was certain it was the Buket Bintang and I was due there at 8 p.m. on Monday evening. On arrival, I enquired if a Mr Lou had booked dinner. The staff informed me that I wanted the Millionaire's Mess which was the penthouse of the hotel. I was directed to the back of the hotel and told to look for a large yellow door to a lift that would take me to the dinning suite. The lift doors opened and a huge Chinaman in traditional Chinese dress appeared in front of me. He stepped out from the lift and asked who I was and what I wanted. I told him that a Mr Lou had invited me to dinner, with that he bowed and made a hand sign for me to enter the lift. At the penthouse landing the doorman pointed to the cloakroom and said, "Pergi di sana" (go there). As I entered the room, two Chinese girls welcomed me, took my clothes off and rubbed me down with scented towels. I was then given a pair of red shorts, a silk dressing gown, slippers and led into the main room. Seated at a large round table were four Chinese, one of which was Mr Lou. I had met him once before when he introduced his manager to me on Sungai Buloh. Mr Lou stood up and made me welcome, introducing the other three Chinese to me. When I sat down the waiter was called and drinks were served.

I had told our Malay sais to come back at 11.30 that evening. However, when he arrived he was dismissed and told to go back to the estate as transport had been arranged for me. Dinner was served at 9 p.m. in real Chinese manner, starting with fruit, sweets, suckling pig and so on. There were 405 courses on the menu. The feasting and drinking, with all kinds of entertainment between courses went on and on. It lasted almost three days! I was taken back to Sungai Buloh in a daze sometime on Wednesday, I think!

I must tell this story, it happened some years back. A well-known foreign correspondent of the era, for a popular Sunday newspaper, wrote an article on a Chinese millionaire's mess in Singapore, I can't remember exactly when, but it was in the late forties or very early fifties. His article went something like this. The correspondent had been invited by a rich Chinese merchant to dine with him at the millionaire's mess and one of the courses was monkey brains, he went on to say, a boy sat below the table with a basket of live monkeys, in the middle of the table was a hole. When the host called for monkey brains he would hold a monkey with its head poking out of the hole. With a large, sharp, knife cleaver, the host would slice off the scalp exposing the brains and the guest would eat the live brains with chopsticks. As this never happened when he dined with the Chinese in their mess, the Chinese merchants were up in arms when the article was published and he had to make a public apology.

In the mid-seventies I joined the Federation of Sussex Industries and was invited to lunch by Dame Nora Potter where I gave a lecture on my Urethane Foam Systems to fellow members. Dame Nora had also invited the foreign correspondent to give an after lunch speech about his life as a journalist. He never mentioned the monkey brains saga and went on to say he had never been sued or been in any trouble during his time as a foreign correspondent. However, after the speech I managed to catch him alone for a minute and told him I was in Malaya when the monkey row took place. All he said was, "For heaven's sake don't mention that please, come and join me in a drink."

I don't believe monkey brains were served at the table during my stay at the Millionaire's Mess in Kuala Lumpur, at least I have no memory of them. I must check that old mess menu, I think I may have it somewhere about.

Bad Luck?

With Malayan Independence due the following year, security in the Selangor area was being scaled down. Personal and factory guards were no longer required, but managers' bungalows, on estates, were still guarded during the night by SP guards. Communist guerrilla activity was now mainly confined to the hinterland, in states like Pahang and Jahore. Daily life was certainly more peaceful and free of constant threat. However things were about to change.

On Sungai Buloh there was a small cottage hospital for any sick member of SME and Strathmore Rubber labour force plus their families. The administration was transferred to Strathairlie Estate when Sungai Buloh was sold. I had taken over the management of Strathairlie the previous month from Mac Hunter. Mac and his wife had departed for six months' home leave. It was here on Strathairlie that I broke my leg in the estate armour-plated Land Rover. There had been a tiger scare in the labour lines and I had been down at the rubber factory with the head mandor looking at some tiger tracks. It was late afternoon and on the way back, just as I approached the bungalow, Mac's dog jumped out of the Land Rover and ran in front of it chasing a squirrel. I had to swerve onto the grass verge. It had been raining that day so the grass was very soft, the verge gave way and the Land Rover turned over and ended up at the bottom of the high bank with me in it.

The SP guard on duty came to my rescue and carried me back to the bungalow. The closest doctor was Dr Anderson, who was in charge of a leper colony some six miles away. I phoned him and he sent over a nursing sister. She gave me first aid and a very welcome injection of morphine. The next morning, I was taken to the hospital in Kuala Lumpur where an X-ray revealed the tibia table on my right leg was split. My entire leg was put in plaster. I learned later this had been the wrong treatment. The cast was covering my foot right up to my crotch. The pressure caused my leg and testicles to swell with fluid and I was in great pain. In the hospital there was a Chinese nursing sister, I had met her on several occasions in the late forties on Sungai Tekal Estate. She often accompanied Dr De Silva when he paid his monthly visit to the labour force. She spoke to me kindly when I was in great pain and advised me to go back home for treatment, which I did.

It took a few days to arrange first class flights home with BOAC as facilities for my condition had to be considered. While waiting for my flight home a navy helicopter pilot was given the bed opposite me. This well-spoken English man turned out to be a great help to me in many ways. He had been brought in to have his collarbone re-set. Piloting a flight carrying three wounded soldiers out of the jungle, the landing and take-off platform of his helicopter had collapsed causing it to crash land on its side. To rescue him, they had to cut through the fuselage and pull him out. In doing so his collarbone had broken. It had healed badly and was misshapen; it needed to be re-set. After his operation the methods used to aid his recovery, I thought, were horrific. Before he regained consciousness I watched as they tied his hands to the top bars and his feet to the bottom bars of the bed. A sandbag was placed over his stomach for good measure. After witnessing this, I was very glad I had booked a flight home!

When the pilot awoke the following morning, he raised his head from the small pillow and said, "What the hell's going on here?" He could hardly move, and called for the nurse to cut him loose. She tried to explain that she could not, without the doctor's permission. When two doctors finally came round, the pilot was told he would need to be kept like this for two weeks! Understandably, the pilot was not pleased and asked the senior doctor to phone a professor in England, who was a family friend, for his advice. To phone the UK in those days you had to book the call, which took about eight hours, if not longer. After the doctors left he was fed, washed, and put to sleep again.

Early the next morning when the Malay orderlies came to work, the pilot asked one of them to cut him loose, but the orderly did not understand, so I translated for the pilot. He was first offered $5 to cut the arm loose, going up at a rate of $5 for each request until the sum of $25 was reached. At that point the orderly was in two minds and was about to cut the arm loose, but had second thoughts and walked away shaking his head. I often wonder if the pilot got his way, no doubt he survived to tell the story.

Last Journey Home

The next day I began the long and painful journey home. I was taken to Kuala Lumpur airport by a taxi ambulance and then flew down to Singapore in a Dakota. From there I went on to the Raffles Hotel by special taxi, where I spent the night. The next morning, after breakfast, the same taxi arrived to take me to the airport where I was put on a BOAC Constellation bound for Karachi, which was an overnight stop. On arrival at Karachi a small baggage train met me off the plane. On the last bogie there was a large rattan chair with a punkah wallah standing by, carrying a large fan! After all the other passengers had disembarked, I was taken off and put in the large chair, with my plastered leg resting on a stool, I was fanned all the way by the punkah wallah to the Terminal hotel. This was first class travel at its best! The next stop was London. On arrival in London, I was the first to be taken off the plane. An ambulance was waiting to take me across the airport to a Britannia aircraft bound for Glasgow Airport. BOAC had planned all these first class flights. In those days, an excellent service from start to finish. When the Britannia landed at Glasgow, Della had hired a taxi and was waiting on the runway to take me home to Kirriemuir.

The next morning I was taken to the Dundee Royal Infirmary by ambulance. The consultant, Mr Smillie, ordered the plaster to be cut off so the knee could be drained. There must have been half a gallon of fluid, if not more. It was a huge relief and once it was drained most of the pain had gone. I wonder what would have happened if I had stayed in Kuala Lumpur for treatment. The surgeon did say, "What idiot ordered that plaster cast?" I am forever grateful to the Chinese nursing sister for her wise advice. I was in hospital for six weeks, 'in traction', after which I had to walk with a calliper attached to the sole of my shoe, for a period of some eight weeks.

Dundee Infirmary

Although the injury never hampered my walking and playing sports, it was never fully recovered and in later years did deteriorate. The complete knee joint was replaced in 1996 and I have had no trouble to date. After this accident I had a strong feeling my luck in Malaya was running out, so I resigned from Scottish Malayan Estates and returned to a new life with Della in Scotland.

Dykes 2006

Dykes 2013

When my own children were young I was able to tell them stories of tigers, elephants and crocodiles, but the memoirs I have written in this book tell the full stories, adversities, tragedies and all. Even with all its trials and dangers, my memories of Malaya are happy ones. I grew to love and respect this beautiful country, its people, their varying beliefs and ways of life. Malaya has always been part of me and will continue to hold a special place in my heart.

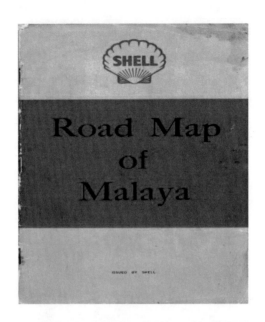

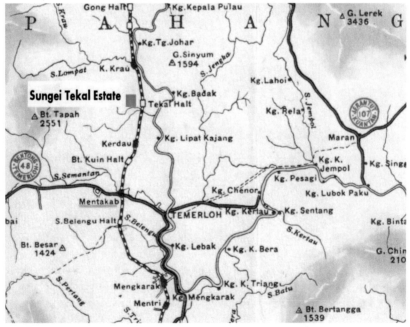

My original map, 1948

Terang Bulan (Bright Moon)
Malay with English translation
Several versions of this song exist this is just one of them

Terang bulan, terang di pinggir kali
Buaya timbul disangkalah mati
Jangan percaya mulutnya lelaki
Berani sumpah 'tapi takut mati

Waktu potong padi di tengah sawah
Sambil bernyanyi riuh rendah
Memotong padi semua orang
Sedari pagi sampai petang

Waktu potong padi di tengah sawah
Sambil bernyanyi riuh rendah
Bersenang hati sambil bersuka
Tolonglah kami bersama sama

ENGLISH TRANSLATION

The moon is shining, moon shine reflects on the river
Floating crocodile thought to be dead
Don't believe man's word
Dare to pledge but afraid of dying

Whilst harvesting paddy in the field
Singing gaily
Everybody is harvesting paddy
morning past to evening (unnoticed)

Whilst harvesting paddy in the field
Singing gaily
Heart at ease while having fun
Help us together

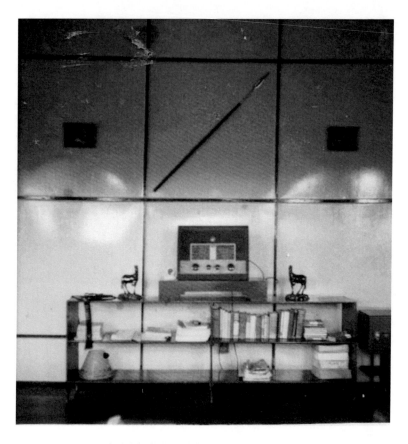

The Living Room at Tekal

APPENDIX A

At the end of WW2 and before the return of the British to Malaya, the MPAJA (Malayan People's Anti-Japanese Army) celebrated the defeat of Japan. In one of their strongholds, Ipoh in Perak, the 5th Independent Regiment 1,000-strong paraded followed by hundreds of MPAJA supporters. In most towns throughout Malaya, MPAJA representatives documented all proceedings including Victory Parades. The celebrations were swiftly followed by the formation of many Malay radical political parties calling for 'Merdeka' (freedom).

Many Pahang Malays had told me that the Japanese were on the verge of giving independence to the Malays when WW2 suddenly ended. The reason for this, in my opinion, may have been to keep their old enemy, the Chinese, at bay. The return of the British was a great disappointment to the Pahang Malays.

The largest party by far, was the Malayan Communist Party, MCP, mainly Chinese. Their leader, Chen Peng, was in full command of the Malayan People's Anti-Japanese Army, 5,000-strong. In this complicated political scene, there was discord and intrigue. Old British Malaya was about to change and change it did with the outbreak of the Emergency.

APPENDIX B

In 2010 at one of our Parachute Regiment meetings in Worthing, I was told that civilians could apply for the Malayan Campaign Medal. I thought for me this would be easy. How wrong I was. Seemingly civilians in the NAAFI, YMCA, Church of Scotland and such like, some of whom may never have seen a Communist Guerrilla, all qualify for the medal. But alas rubber planters, many who fought off the onslaught of the Communist Army from the early months of 1948, 'are not eligible for the award'. Whoever said that, 'The Civil Service was half full of half-wits', may have had a point. See medal office copy letter.

Service Personnel
& Veterans Agency
An Executive Agency of the Ministry of Defence

Ministry of Defence Medal Office
Imjin Bks
Innsworth
GLOUCESTER
GL3 1HW
Tel: 0141 224 3600
Email: Medals@SPVA.mod.uk

Mr C Aitkenhead
8 Elm Park
Ferring
West Sussex
BN12 5RW

Ref: SPVA/MODMO/ARMY/
        HISTORIC/1675892

Date: 3 December 2009

MEDAL ENTITLEMENT

Dear Mr Aitkenhead

Thank you for your letter dated 11 November 2009.

The General Service Medal (1918) with clasp Malaya is awarded for service in the Federation of Malaya between 16 June 1948 and 31 July 1960, or in Singapore between 16 June 1948 and 31 January 1959. In order to qualify civilians had to have served as a member of one of the following approved categories:

British Red Cross Society and Order of St John
War Department Physiotherapists sent out from the UK who wore British Red Cross uniform
NAAFI Staff
WRVS
SSAFA
YMCA
YWCA
Church of Scotland Huts Committee
Army Scripture Readers Association

We regret to inform you that as an employee of Rubber Plantations you are not eligible for the award.

We are sorry to give you what may be a disappointing reply.

Yours sincerely

M J Harwood
MODMO
for Chief Executive

APPENDIX C

Chop Teck Seng

In 1984 Della and I had a long holiday in the Far East visiting Hong Kong, Java, Bali and during the holiday we spent three weeks in Malaya. There is now a government road to Sungai Tekal Estate running alongside the Malayan Siam railway. The young Chinese manager of Sungai Tekal Estate was very obliging when we met him but knew nothing about what happened in the past (1948) on Sungai Tekal. Before leaving the estate we visited the labour lines, unfortunately most of the labour force was out at work. As far as the labour quarters were concerned nothing much had changed. However I spoke to an elderly women in Tamil and she answered me back in Malay. Between Tamil and Malay I learned that the labour force that I knew had long gone, much to my disappointment. From there we went on to Mentakab to visit my old Chinese friend Chop Teck Seng. We went to his old premises but were told he was now a Towkay Besar (rich merchant) and had offices and shops in the main street. We went to his new premises and I asked female assistant if I could see Chop Teck Seng. With that a Chinese gentleman rushed out shouting, "Mr Aitkenhead, Mr Aitkenhead." I asked him who he was, he replied, "Don't you remember me, I am Teck Seng's son, you gave me an Easter egg when I was seven years old." When I asked about his father he told me he had passed away the year before. He added that it was a great honour my remembering his father after all these years. I replied, "How could I forget him, he was my friend."

During our conversation, over an ice cool beer, he insisted that we join him and his family for diner that evening. He suggested we should dine from the vendors in the street. In this small town there was one part of the main street where all the restaurants were on the menu. One restaurant specialised in duck another in pork, another in fish and so on. The street was cleared of all traffic and set out with a selection of round tables. The previous day we had booked into a hotel in Temerloh some ten miles from Mentakab. That evening as arranged, a large car was sent to pick us up. We drove to Mentakab where a rickshaw was waiting to take us to Teck Seng's table in the street, where we met his family. Della was made guest of honour and sat between Teck Seng's mother and his wife. When a waiter was called from one of the kedai makan (restaurants), the waiter held his hand over his mouth when he spoke, and all other waiters did the same, so that their breath could not be inhaled by guests. This was a very old Chinese custom. The excellent meal was served with all the Chinese traditional manners. Della, being guest of honour, was served first by Teck's mother and his wife. There was also a drinks waiter standing by – we never saw the bottom of our glass. This was Chinese hospitality at its best. It was an honour for Della and I to have been the fortunate recipients. After the dinner we were taken back to our hotel in the same luxurious manner.

The next day we went back to Mentakab to thank and bid farewell to Teck Seng and his family. After this, Della wanted to have her hair done at a hairdresser's, so we found a salon. However, the girl in the salon could not speak English, so I translated. While Della was having her hair done, the salon assistant kept bringing me cups of coffee and showing me large photos of Marilyn Monroe with different hairstyles and asking me if Della would like one. When we went to pay the bill, we were told it was on Teck Seng's account. Later in a Chinese hardware shop I bought a Chinese cleaver and again I was told that it was to be put on Teck Seng's account. It was now time to get back to our hotel in Temerloh to pack. When I went to pay the hotel bill, the same thing happened, it was already covered by Teck Seng. Teck Seng now owned rubber plantations and during dinner had offered me a post as General Manager. This may have been the reason for his generosity. If I had been younger I may have taken up his offer!

INDEX

A
Abdullah CD. 27
Aborigines 96,121
Agricultural Research Dept. 91
Ah Sek, Sam 102,103
Airlie estate 14,48
Ali, Wan 37,38
Ayah (Thomson household) 51,52

B
Bank of India Australia & China 27
Bedford Estate 58,59
Bentong 70,71,101,122,123
Blood Brother 44,46,47
blood money 96
Bomah/Pawang 43,61
boring beetles 69
Bourne, General 103

Bright Moon (Terang bulan) 39,141
buffalo 82,83
Bukit Bintang Hotel 42
Bukit Cheraka estate 14,18,19,23
Bukit Hantu 109, 111
Burma Railway 13,55,64,65
Burns, Robert 97
bat guano 109,111
Batu Melintang 86

C
Chong,Ah 102 -105
Chuan, Ah 101
Climate21,25,39,61,83,100
cobra 91
Creeper 20,41
crocodile 58 -61,90,139

D
Danish planter 61,62

147

Diwali Festival 96,97,98
Dogs, hunting 78 - 81
Douglas,Lord 16
Dundee Royal Infirmary   137,138

E
Eagle (lang) 89
Edinburgh 13,14
electrical storms 94,95
Elephant (Gajah) 23,92,93,94,139
Elmina estate 24,38 - 43,48,50 -56,87,101
Esk, river 130
European Cemetery 54
European & Orient Hotel 17

F
Film Club 74 -78, 96,98,105,118
Force 136   46,110

G
Gallipoli 11
Gemas 24,64,65
Genting highlands 122
George Hotel Edinburgh 13
Gurkhas 34,72,80,82 -86,103
Geruda (eagle of the gods) 89,110,111,114
Glamis estate 11,115,130

H
Hampshire Regiment 99
Haram 27
Hari Raya Buaya (crocodile festival)61,83
Harrods 128,129
Hashim 46
Herd, Angus 13
Hens 87,89,93,102,106
Hickman, John 100,102,103,106,107
Highland games 75,129,130
Hindu Temple 91,97,98,115
Hislop MC 80,94
Hunt,Major General 15

I
ICI 94,111
Iguana 50,78,88,111
Independent 32nd Platoon   96,101,102
Indian Army 13,45,79
Indian Film Unit 74
Invulnerability cults 37

J
jahat (wicked/evil) 61
Jahore 65,135
Japanese Indonesian Army 36
Japanese occupation of Malaya27,40,50,65,110
Justinhaugh Hotel 130,132

K
Ka Sim, Woo 95,96,105
keluang (fruit bat) 109
Kelantan 41,43,67,87, 37
Kemut Berahi 41
Kangany 80,81
kerani (clerk)92
Kerdau 70,101,102,106
Kirriemuir (Kirrie)11,13,14,21,46,48,55,63,70,71,115,127-133,137
Koon, Kaw 101
Kota Bharu 41,64
Kuala Krau 26,34,37,47,82,85,86,89,101,109 - 111,120
Kuala Lumpar 93
Kut-al-Almara 13

L
Lallang 94
Lang (eagle) 89
Lee, Chan 89,90
Luger pistol 47

M
Malta 16
Malabar Coast 97,115,116